THE MILL HOUSE
AND THEREABOUTS

Also available in this series:

The Mill House and Thereabouts

Recollections of an idyllic childhood in Sprowston, Norfolk

by

Wing Commander H. C. Harrison A.R.C.Sc., O.B.E.

Line drawings by Graham R. Nesbit and W. Pyne

ISIS
LARGE PRINT
Oxford and Orlando

First published in Great Britain 1998
by The Larks Press

Published in Large Print 2000 by ISIS Publishing Ltd,
7 Centremead, Osney Mead, Oxford OX2 0ES, and
ISIS Publishing, PO Box 195758,
Winter Springs, Florida 32719-5758, USA
by arrangement with The Larks Press

British Library Cataloguing in Publication Data
Harrison, H. C. (Herbert Clifford), b. 1888
 The mill house and thereabouts: recollections of an idyllic
childhood in Sprowston, Norfolk. – Large print ed.
 1. Harrison, H. C. (Herbert Clifford), b. 1888 – Childhood and
youth 2. Large type books 3. Sprowston (Norfolk, England)
– Rural conditions 4. Sprowston (Norfolk, England) – Social
conditions – 19th century
 I. Title
 942.6'1'081

ISBN 0-7531-5787-X (hb)
ISBN 0-7531-5788-8 (pb)

Printed and bound by Antony Rowe, Chippenham and Reading

DEDICATION

To my Grand-daughters:

Janet Leuwin Harrison
Margaret Susan Harrison
Judith Elizabeth Harrison

Will you look upon this book as your very own. It tells as well as I am able, of events in what to each of you is a distant time and a distant clime.

Some day, perhaps, a ship that sails the ocean wide will carry you to England. If that should come about, you will go to that corner of it that the book speaks of. There, if you but half close your eyes, you may glimpse the quiet days that your grandparents lived and their grandparents before them.

For it is surely remarkable that, whereas your Daddy's people were farmers at Overstrand and millers at Sprowston, some of your mother's people came from lovely Thorpe, the very next village to Sprowston. This, in their generation, they did not know until after they had met and married here in Australia.

So you, my dears, have roots there which reach through history to the Iceni and beyond.

BABA

This book was written in 1948 and has been published at the instigation of the author's son, the late Mr Hubert C. Harrison of Melbourne, Australia.

PREFACE

I was born in the Mill House — the third Harrison to begin existence there. I was preceded by a sister (Edith) and a brother (Willie) and was to be followed by two more brothers (Horace and Leonard) and finally another sister (Olive) — a compact family of six.

No Harrison had been born there previously and none will be again.

And yet the mill and the Mill House had been in the family for generations. That came about because my father took over the mill at the death of a maternal uncle, George Robertson; he was, therefore, the first Harrison to live at the Mill House and to work the mill.

If the mill was not built by a Robertson, it must have come into the possession of the family shortly afterwards. It was the custom of successive owners to engrave their initials on the massive central post, and the date of entering into possession. The Robertson initials dated from the year 1780, but the first of that name we heard my father speak of was his grandfather, Robert Robertson, who came to the mill about 1830, and met his death by an accident in it. He had a family of three sons, all of whom became millers, and three daughters.

Of the Robertson sisters, Elizabeth married a farmer — William Harrison. Except that the family vault is at Sprowston, little seems to be known of them, only that William continued as a farmer in a number of Norfolk villages — Oby, Blofield, Ormesby and Limpenhoe. They had a family of eight. The first was a daughter and then came a succession of seven sons. My grandmother would often speak whimsically of them as the "seven wonders". Four of them became millers.

My father was the third son. In early life, he had no prospect or intention of becoming a miller. He had gone to London and was embarked upon the building hardware business. My mother — a Norfolk girl — was engaged to him at this time, but I have heard her say that he declared he would not marry until he had a business of his own. When George Robertson died, Sprowston Mill was offered to my father; he had the hard decision to make as to whether to remain in the hardware business, in which he had good prospects, or to accept the offer of Sprowston knowing nothing whatever about millering. Perhaps my mother persuaded him, seeing that at Sprowston he would immediately become the owner of his own business.

However, come to Sprowston he did, and fulfilled his promise to my mother in 1884. They lived there long enough to celebrate the golden anniversary of their wedding but, after the mill was burnt down in 1933, they retired to Lowestoft and there celebrated their diamond anniversary.

The mill was burnt down in somewhat dramatic circumstances on March 24th, 1933, the day before it was to have been formally taken over as an "ancient building" by the Norfolk Archaeological Trust. My father has said that he would never have left the Mill House whilst the mill was standing but it was so much a part of his life and being, that he did not wish to stay after it was gone. For him the landscape was empty.

Sprowston, then, was the traditional home of the Robertsons, and the Mill House was so regarded by the succeeding generation — that of the Harrisons — in spite of the fact that the third son was in occupation and not the eldest. This probably accounts for the frequent visits of cousins, uncles and aunts.

Millers and farmers, of course, worked very closely together. The miller bought his wheat from the farmer and gristed his fodder grain for him. We youngsters, therefore, had many friends amongst the farmers' children and could as easily be taken for budding farmers as budding millers. In the full leaf of after years only one of us (Horace) became either — and he a farmer.

Those early days were indeed placid; life flowed at an even tenor, as it can never do again. Everything appeared to be so utterly stable. One learnt at school that there had been a national crisis as far back as 1066, and several others since. But to children, that was only history to be read in books; such things did not happen nowadays. Victoria had been Queen of England almost since living memory — a most excellent arrangement. True, England did go to war — the Boer War — and many men from our own village of Sprowston volunteered to engage in it. But it was remote and impersonal and in nowise entered into the scheme of life.

And, looking back, what an extraordinary period in which to live. The bracket of years which we have embraced in our lives has included so many things which would have appeared absolutely fantastic at the beginning of it. Electricity was almost non-existent outside the laboratory. The whole development of electric lighting, heating, railway traction, telephones and the wizardry of wireless and radar was to come and so with the motor vehicle, astronomy, agriculture, the whole science of aeronautics, even nuclear fission. Where does one stop?

And still it is not a life-span since these things did not exist. We have to go back but a few years to see what life was like without them.

CONTENTS

The Mill Lane

On the outskirts of the City of Norwich lies Mousehold — a name which invariably intrigues the stranger. He wants to call it "Mousehole" and is puzzled to know how such a large expanse of heath could take its name from such an insignificant creature. In truth, of course, it does not; its name is derived from its association with men and not mice. When, in the days of the Conqueror, Norwich was the second city in the Kingdom, it contained within its boundaries a monastery, far-famed for its learning. The monks pastured their sheep and kine in the lush meadows bordering the river which flowed in a wide sweep around their demesne. They also laid claim to the rough heath country on the uplands beyond the river's bank. This was then the monks' holding — Monks' Hold — a name which easily became transmuted in the passage of centuries into the present-day rendering of "Mousehold".

Today you may roam the valleys and hillocks of the heath, brushing through the heather which almost obscures the narrow tracks, and come to that high ground overlooking the old city. Kett's Hill it is now called and from here you survey those same meadows in which the monks toiled in bygone years, the Cathedral with its delicate spire pointing to the sky, and beyond, the rugged Norman Castle with battlemented parapets, standing foursquare over the expanse of the city.

The Mill House stood over against the Heath, not directly adjoining it. You could reach it — in unorthodox fashion certainly — by going first to the Mill Hill and from there to the Top Meadow.

At one place you could squeeze through the hawthorn hedge which brought you into the broken area where clay for brickmaking was excavated. Threading your way through deep gulches and over scattered mounds you could clamber up the other side and be on the Heath in five minutes or so from the outset.

But, in the ordinary way, you do not approach the Mill House from Mousehold. You come in towards Norwich by the main road leading from Broadland — the Wroxham Road. Exactly one mile from the old city gate is the turning into the mill lane which leads up past the house to the mill hill beyond. So narrow it is that the teamster delivering corn to the mill is faced with a most delicate manoeuvre, calling for all his skill, in negotiating his big farm wagon from the road into the lane. The four powerfully built horses rest in their traces as he stops them in the road at the bottom of the lane. He climbs down from his high seat, and makes a survey of the sweep he will have to take. He judges it carefully from this side and the other. Yes, it is just possible. Back in his seat again he gathers up his team, gives a flick to the reins, and they swing the wagon into the entrance. There can be no halting now. It looks as if the off-side

2

leader will be driven clean through the hedge in the lane, but the turn is made safely, although so finely was it judged that only a cat's whisker separated the near-side wheel from disaster against the stone wall. Once in the lane the gradient calls for free action from the horses until they are whoa-ed up right by the side of the Mill House looking into the windows of the dining room.

There is no heavier traffic — no more majestic vehicle on the road — than the farmer's wagon. The building of it took many months of patient and honest work on the part of the local wheelwright and wagon builder. The oaken timbers, every one, have been selected from a stock that has been seasoning for years. They are well and truly morticed. The spacious body is upswept at the front to lines which are pleasing to the eye and which provide a commanding position for the wagoner's seat. The flared sides are stiffened with ornate strouters. Elm, oak, and ash go into the making of hub, spokes, and fellies of wheels, built high and wide against the hazards of rutted roads.

The wagoner, sturdy and hale, quiet and considerate with his horses, confident in the handling of his wagon through narrow country lanes and gateways, is every inch a craftsman. His craftsmanship comes to him through living under the open sky and close to the soil in daily heed of creatures who do the same. He moves around but little from his native village; indeed this journey of some four miles to the mill is almost the fullest extent of his travels. It is sufficient of an event that in the evening he will recount his day's experiences over a pint of ale.

On this summer's day his coat is off and his blue shirt is open at the neck. His hat is of straw, such as the reapers wear at haysel and harvest, but when he comes to the mill in winter, he will put an empty corn sack over his shoulders against the searching wind and another one over his knees. He will wear a cap which he himself has made from many skins of the small field vole — always to be exterminated wherever its earth-mounds appear. If the weather is cold and the wind keen, he will draw down the lug-flaps and button them under his chin to protect his ears. His legs will be encased in soft skin buskins buttoned-on over his trouser legs. When he stands to talk, his hands slip easily into the front pockets of his breeches to be warmed by the warmth of his stomach.

At Christmas time he and the miller will confer on the matter of largesse — a payment which comes to him by right of entitlement for service to the mill throughout the year and must never be confused with a gratuity which the miller might or might not withhold. He "puts in for his larges" with squared shoulders and level eyes and is met by the miller on those same terms.

Today he has yet to get his wagon to the mill hill from where he stopped by the Mill House. The gradient of this part of the lane is much steeper. As his horses stand and take their breather, they are a little perturbed at what goes on in the direction of the mill. Perhaps they catch sight of the swinging sails, or more probably, judging from the way they occasionally cock an ear, they hear the swish of the wind in them.

But breather time is over and now it is to work again. The wagoner has already been up on to the mill hill to see what space he will have there. At the same time, he called to the miller and told him that he had a load of corn to deliver. As he stands now by his wagon, he casts another glance at the steep hill and then makes ready. Quietly he goes round his team, a friendly smack for this one, a stern "steady" to that — the harness, the traces, the axle pins, all is in order. The horses know that they are about to move off and shuffle impatiently whilst awaiting the word for action. The miller fetches a large wedge-shaped chock and takes position behind the rear wheels in readiness to sprag them in case the grade becomes too severe. The wagoner climbs to his seat and collects the reins. He knows that his load is over four tons, that in the next half minute, before the top of the hill is breasted, each of his horses will have to work, not with the power of one, but of ten.

And now a firmness on the reins, and the word for action comes; strongly, but quietly, at first; "Buster, gid-up, Jeannie, Blackie, gid-up, h-ey-e there", and then in full cry: "GID-UP, GID-UP, BUSTER, BLONDIN, HI, HI, GID-UP".

Rarely has the voice they know well held such a tone of urgency — of determination. Down go four heads as the bodies lean forward to take the strain. Sixteen huge hooves bite into the gravel and the wagon gathers way. The wagoner watches every movement, watches the shaggy manes swaying as the heads swing low to the strenuous effort up and down, up and down, the fore-feet striking one after the other. Are the leaders flagging: — Buster, Blondin, the tracers: Jeannie, Blackie. And so to the top: — "STEADY, steady,

WHOA-A." Had they stalled half-way, there would have been no prospect of getting started again. In such plight the wagon must be unloaded where it stood and the work then was back-breaking.

Heaving flanks and dilated nostrils tell that they use every ounce they had. Presently their mentor hitches up the reins and climbs down. To each in turn he goes and looks him over, giving a word or pat of encouragement as he passes to the next. Especially does he watch for a loosened shoe, for the heavy going puts the farrier's work to an extreme test. However, everything is well. Now they can set about unloading the wagon comfortably.

There is little room on the mill hill for manoeuvring with a full team so he unhitches the leaders and takes them to the top meadow; then he drives his wagon the few yards to the unloading wicket in the roundhouse. Both he and the miller are used to handling sacks of 14 stone weight and the job proceeds apace.

If you approach the Mill House from the direction of Norwich, the turn into the mill lane is just as sharp as it is from the opposite direction. Various vehicles come from Norwich — merchants' lorries, railway vans, and tradesmen's carts. None of them are four-horse vehicles like the farm wagon and they make the turn into the mill lane without difficulty — all except one.

That singular vehicle is driven by the squire of an outlying village who has been to the city and has a call to make upon the miller on the way home. He drives an extremely high dog-cart — a beautifully finished thing gleaming with highly polished varnish. The ultra-high wheels are built with spindly spokes and the narrowest of rims. The double seat is perched high; the shafts are mere willow wands. It is the lightest of vehicles built. The driver sits very erect with the reins properly fingered in the left hand — the long decorative whip held at the correct angle across the body in the right. His groom sits behind him immovable with arms folded. To draw this splendid equipage, two horses are harnessed in tandem. More elbow grease than dubbin has gone into their harness to bring up the rich russet tone that sets it aglow. Every buckle shines brightly. They are magnificent animals, sleek and fine and groomed to perfection; even their hooves have been polished with shoeshine. Both are subjected to the restraint of a bearing rein so that progress is made in high stepping fashion with necks well arched. In keeping with the general striking appearance of the turn-out, the leader is harnessed in long tandem; that is to say, the length of his traces stations him well ahead of the trace horse. It is partly this which leads to the difficulty in making the turn into the mill lane. As they slow for the turn, the leader wants to go straight along the road towards home as he more frequently does — and by the time he is persuaded that is not the general idea, he is crosswise to the road, not opposite the lane. Eventually, after much ineffective coaxing, the groom jumps down and leads him into the lane — a most undignified proceeding as applied to the art of tandem driving.

Once in the lane the groom leaps up to his seat again so that they may reach the Mill House in faultless style. When the miller comes up, which he does almost

7

immediately — for it would be unpardonable to keep this splendid turn-out waiting — the talk is of feed for the horses. Are the new season's oats suitably matured yet? Will they not gripe the animals? Has he any of last year's harvest left for the younger ones?

Meanwhile, the tandem team paws the ground and frets on the bearing rein. Time and again the leader rears up on to his hind legs and several times it looks as though he will finish up with his hooves through the dining-room window. The master is not greatly concerned, however, and presently he turns them about and, to everyone's relief, they set off down the lane again. If, as seen from behind, the groom's shoulders appear to relax their rigidity ever so little, it must be because of his knowledge that to him would have fallen the task of extricating them from broken glass and window frames had the leader's restlessness grown much more.

The doctor's brougham made the turn into the mill lane on seven occasions for the purpose of introducing a new member to the family, and on such other occasions as were necessary to ensure that he or she stayed in it. Once he was not successful.

Actually, I believe there must have been times at night when he did not drive up in his brougham because, in the absence of telephones, the only way of getting him quickly was to drive into Norwich and fetch him. I can scarcely imagine, however, any case so desperate that such a happening could be countenanced in the daytime. The brougham was so distinctive and professional with its cockaded coachman on the box seat. It was a firm ritual at the Mill House that THE DOCTOR should never be kept waiting at the door for an instant. As the brougham drove into the mill lane, the maid would be called to take post at the front door ready to open it immediately his foot came to the doorstep. To us children the sight of his top hat and gloves on the hall table whilst he was upstairs was awe-inspiring indeed. The whispered word went round — "The doctor is here" — and the brougham would be subjected to a still more minute scrutiny through the window, until the great man came down and took his seat and drove away.

He was a most distinguished looking man. Tall and handsome in appearance with a highly waxed moustache. He was always in morning dress — immaculate from top hat to lacquered boots that glistened below his suede spats. He was reserved but friendly in his bedside manner, and his beautifully modulated voice itself gave the patient tremendous courage and an inspiration to recover. We children regarded him as an infallible oracle. There was a certain distrust about home remedies; perhaps the assurances that went with them — "It will make you so much better" — were over-emphasised. But the doctor's word was law unquestioned. I am quite sure that if he had prescribed witches' brew straight from the cauldron, we should have swallowed it down as though it had been the elixir of life itself.

Vehicular Traffic

The open road, the King's Highway: its attraction is never-ending. Around the bend, what may there be? Over the hill an unexplored country lies. Few there are in this age of petrol and pneumatic tyres, who have not heard its call.

There have been changes since those years, round about the beginning of the century, but it is curious to reflect that the main network of roads was laid out by a previous generation. The actual mileage of highway has not increased very much in later years except for the construction of some few arteries and detours.

The roads, I think, were more enchanting then. They have suffered since by the cutting back of high hedges, the smoothing out of odd corners, and even by the change in colour of the surface to a uniform black — all things which have made them not quite so picturesque as they used to be.

Let us go back. The choice of the traveller lay between the railway and some form of horse-drawn vehicle. On the roads there was a sparse service of Barkis-driven carrier vans which plied to the city from outlying villages perhaps twice a week. They were more concerned with the carriage of goods and parcels than with the transport of people; the most they could carry in the way of human freight was one or two passengers seated up beside the driver. And even so, of course, the parcels had still to be collected at various points of call along the route, while the passenger sat waiting. So, it was neither quick nor easy to move about except for people living close to the railway station and, in fact, village people travelled very little. Local customs and manner of speech, therefore, remained uncorrupted by contact with the habits of other places.

Upon reaching the city, the carrier made his rendezvous at one of the old-established hostelries. No longer did the stage coach rattle over the cobbled yard: no longer did the coachman's horn clear the way ahead as ostlers gave freshened horses their lead through the gateway. But some faint glimmer of that past glory lingered on in the bustle of activity which pervaded the hostelry on market days. Farmers and merchants who drove into the city "put up" at the same inn as the carrier, and conducted their business in the bar parlour over a pewter pot. The ostler's role now was to take over the reins from them, unharness and water the horses, and have the gig or dogcart in readiness again when the owner was ready to depart.

Out from the city went another journeyman. His vehicle was also a covered van, but he travelled at a much more leisurely pace than the carrier. Possibly he might not return for weeks. For within his travelling emporium he had stowed a veritable plethora of those domestic articles that pleased the country housewife, from needles to nutmeg, from tape to towels. Even the outside was hung about with the more bulky brooms, baskets and saucepans.

His progress was unhurried. His customers were to be found in every village along the broad highway, yet no byway was too secluded if his wares would find favour there with farmer's wife or cottager's. The children ran to tell of his arrival and stood around fascinated as he made display of ribbons and laces, using the tailboard of the van as an improvised counter.

In contrast to his leisured ways another traveller there was, however, to whom the milestones spoke in tones of urgency. To him they were as the hands of a clock whose signal he dared not disregard. His steed was a spirited colt, his vehicle a light two-wheeled van with doors locked fast. Its red paintwork made it conspicuous against the green roadside hedges. Upon either side was emblazoned in letters of gold, the commanding insignia — "VR". He was the courier carrying Her Majesty's mail.

His time of arrival at the village post-office-cum-store was known to the minute. Whatever the custom in groceries as the hour drew nigh, it must await the closure of the mail bag and the ritual of applying the large medallion of sealing-wax. The letters within bore but a penny stamp — or a half-penny if unsealed — but they now became Her Majesty's Mail and the mail went through on the minute.

In summer, there was somewhat more traffic on the roads, for then there were excursions at weekends and sometimes in midweek, from the city to the country. The big high charabancs — mostly drawn by two horses, though occasionally by three — carried from twenty to thirty people, sitting along either side, facing inwards. Three or four others climbed to a coveted position on the high cross-seat in front alongside the driver. On a Sunday, they passed the Mill House at irregular intervals early in the day, bound for a picnic place by the Broads at Wroxham or Horning Ferry. Returning in the dusk of evening they followed home, one after another, having spun out the day to the utmost limit permitted by the driver.

They all sang themselves home; some charabancs in boisterous fashion according to the degree of stimulation they had drawn from demijohn refreshment; others in sweetest madrigal and roundelay, to the accompaniment of the clip-clop of horses' hooves and the jingling of harness. After a glorious day in the country, the homecoming was not the least of its delights.

The cottagers standing by their garden gates in the gathering twilight waved them on their way with much merriment and the exchange of friendly pleasantries; and each gave as good as he received. Gaiety and good humour pervaded the twilight of a summer's evening until the last stragglers hurried past and were gone. Simple joys they were, but all in keeping with the placid tenor of the times.

To us youngsters at the Mill House, the charabancs were a passing spectacle to be watched from the front meadow. There was never any question of our joining them, because the excursions were organised in the city by various clubs and societies in which country people had no part.

There came another user of the highway. He did not travel in joyous company; he travelled alone — his vehicle the penny-farthing bicycle.

To see him pedalling along, perched high up over the penny wheel, was to wonder however he got started in the first place, how he was going to get down as eventually he must, and, even more, however he learned to ride at all.

If he was a skilled cyclist, he mounted his machine from behind. By reaching forward, he could just grasp the handlebars while he put one foot on the lower step near the ground by the farthing wheel. He then shoved off, scooter fashion, for a few yards until he had enough way on to preserve balance. A quick movement brought his trailing foot to the upper step and from there — heigh-ho — he vaulted to the saddle. The less experienced cyclist faced whatever ignominy might come and sought the advantage of a five-barred gate or the bank of a hedgerow from which to mount — a much less spectacular performance but one which enabled him to reach the seat with greater certainty.

Once in the saddle, and while all went well, he sat there serenely enough, with an outlook upon the road from his high seat all unknown to the mere pedestrian.

The turn at the corner was always a delicate manoeuvre. His legs reached down to the pedals on either side of the penny wheel and, if he steered it round too sharply, his feet would be thrown clear of them and disaster would follow. There were other hazards aplenty. He was so nearly balanced over the wheel that if he leant too far forward to gain advantage in his pedalling, he did

14

so at the peril of taking a header over it. The same peril might come upon him from an unexpected pothole in the road. He had to be particularly careful in windy weather because being perched so high, he was most unstable. Well might the successor to the penny-farthing be called the safety bicycle.

His machine boasted no such thing as ball bearings to reduce the effort of pedalling, and no pneumatic tyres to cushion him from the road. If it was an old model — a bone shaker — it would be fitted with plain iron rims. Only the later and more luxurious makes rejoiced in a solid rubber tyre, formed by wrapping a length of that material round the rim and fastening the ends with a wire fastener. Punctures, of course, were unheard of, but solid rubber tyres had troubles of their own, as would be plain enough should the fastener break and compel the rider to complete his journey on foot with a few yards of tyre draped over his shoulder.

And so you met him — a lone traveller on the road. His speed was very moderate — some ten to twelve miles per hour at most, and the length of his journey was not likely to be more than five or six miles. True, there were more hardy souls who might sometimes make a longer excursion, but neither the state of the roads nor the strenuous pedalling effort involved was an encouragement to them. Only those possessed of an exceptionally tough constitution were able to endure such trials.

Towards the end of the century, however, Dunlop had the vision that it would be possible to "ride on air" and others had developed the art of drawing steel to the form of a thin-walled tube. The solid iron frame of the penny-farthing could now be replaced with a structure that was almost featherweight in comparison and it could be well-insulated from road-shock. Yet it was the development of the light high-duty chain which made it possible to do away with the large diameter wheel of the penny-farthing, for then the machine could be geared so that the pedals turned much more slowly than the wheels. Wire wheels and ball bearings added their contribution to the success of the new machine.

With the invention of the new safety bicycle, the penny-farthing at once became old-fashioned and soon disappeared altogether. Consequently there was really no need to distinguish it by the name of "safety bicycle". It soon became abbreviated to what was originally very much a slang term — "bike".

Older folk, who had no occasion to ride, did not like the new bicycle at all. Such a fast and silent machine was a menace to life and limb. And of those who did want to ride, there were quite a few who could not accept that word "safety". The thing was certainly not so high as the penny-farthing, but you still had to mount it from the step fixed to the hub, and again, having but two wheels, it had little more stability than its predecessor. The fact that you would fall from a lesser height did not persuade them that it merited its title.

The tricycle, therefore, came to satisfy these more doubting ones. We who are so used to wheels from childhood days, find it difficult to realise that here was a generation that had never known them. To them it was putting an unwarranted trust in Providence to expect to retain your balance on two wheels of whatever size. So for them there was the tricycle although it was more expensive and went neither very fast nor very far.

The safety bicycle sprang into popularity for other reasons. The penny-farthing cyclist travelled alone — his was not a sociable machine; whereas the safety cyclist could ride in company anywhere, since most of his companions were possessed of a machine like his own. Indeed, the manufacturers made an attempt to exploit this idea still further, first with the tandem which has never quite died away; and later with the side-by-side machine where the two riders sat one on either side of the frame, each with his own handlebars and pedals, so that neither of them had a permanent view of his companion's back.

Again, there was the basket-work trailer in which the stout-hearted cyclist towed his elderly relative. His share in the proceedings was most unenviable; poor man, he could only bend his head well down over the handlebars and exert himself to the point of exhaustion whilst his passenger reclined in queenly comfort in the trailer — a situation which would have little appeal nowadays to either tower or towed. The combination, in fact, could scarcely be regarded as a sociable arrangement.

So far, however, cycling was not an enterprise for women. The decorum of the day decreed that a woman's skirts should sweep the ground; limbs there might be, but not legs — and hardly ankles. A few daring ones tackled the situation by contriving elastic appurtenances which kept their skirts under some sort of control as they pedalled along; even so, they invited the caustic comment of their more conservative sisters. Daring even more greatly were those who threw convention to the winds and adopted the "rational" dress — a garment very similar to the present-day masculine golfer's plus-fours. They were few in number and quite frequently would find it necessary, if they ventured to the city, to take refuge in a shop to escape being mobbed by astounded spectators. Now that a woman may wear anything from trunks to trousers without so much as an eyebrow being raised in her direction, it is the more difficult to realise the trials of the early pioneer.

Not that these frivolities worried the younger generation. The growing girl rode her bicycle with her brothers and thereby enjoyed a freedom and an outlook upon life that her mother had never known.

We youngsters lived in that transition period when for a number of years the roads belonged almost exclusively to the cyclist. There were no motor cars — not any; they had not yet been invented, or at least had not been developed to such a stage of reliability that they could be taken on a journey over country roads. We were just young enough to remember the penny-farthing but, by the time we were nine or ten years old, the safety bicycle had become well established and each of us had our own. When cousins came to stay, it was a simple matter to hire an extra machine from a cycle depot in the City.

There is a sweep of the Norfolk coastline from Lowestoft to Cromer which forms roughly a circular arc, having Norwich as its centre. At the Mill House we were only very slightly displaced from that central point. To reach the sea, therefore, we had an almost equal choice, as far as distance was concerned, of any one of several radial routes. When we older ones were quite small it was an annual treat to make a family expedition by road to the sea. The mode of conveyance was the horse-drawn gig and that determined that Sea Palling was always selected as the spot to be visited because, being the shortest route to the sea, it was the least tiring to the horse and gave us all a longer day on the coast. Even so, it involved a drive of 40 or 50 miles there and back. The excursion was an event of the year and took more than a little arranging between the three or four families who joined in. We had pleasurable anticipations of it for weeks ahead.

And then what a change — a few years later — when we had our bicycles. We could as easily reach the wind-swept sand dunes at Sea Palling, the cliffs at Mundesley or Cromer or the crowded sands at Yarmouth or Lowestoft. On highdays and holidays, the bicycles would be brought out soon after breakfast. Invariably, there were last-minute repairs and adjustments to be made. Someone amongst the party would have a doubtful tyre to mend — (it would be in no less doubtful condition after it had been mended) — a sloppy wheel to be tightened; a saddle to be adjusted more comfortably. Oil can and tyre pump would pass from hand to hand. Parents would be hovering around joining in cheerfully with the preparations and offering suggestions intended to be helpful.

At last all the screwing up is finished and everyone is ready to take to the road. Light-hearted as they are, the caution to take care which is called to them as they ride away falls on unheeding ears. It is dismissed in the general wave of farewell. The whole bright day lies before them; cares of any description do not enter into their plans for the enjoyment of it.

And indeed the road is open with scarcely a vestige of any other wheeled traffic and, of course, no motor vehicles whatsoever. Few dangers can come upon them unless through carelessness arising from their own high-spirited jubilation.

On such days as these there is no firm intention of following any set course; rather the familiar tracks are avoided so that the expedition may have the added spice of exploration.

Their way takes them through unfrequented by-ways where the high hedgerows are redolent of the perfume of sweetbriar and honeysuckle; where the stillness of the soft calm morning lies like a haze over the quiet countryside; where the lightest sound carries afar. From a distance the voices of the cottagers' children ring vibrant through the dulcet air. Their light laughter intermingles with other sounds of activity around the cottage — the creak of their father's barrow as he goes about tending his vegetable patch, the rattle of water pails which his wife sets without the door to be filled from the well. All are softened and blended into the morning's tranquil harmony.

As the bicycles come near to the cottage, the children gaze at them, shy and demure, from the gateway, for they meet with few strangers in their placid world. A friendly "Hello" may send them retiring within the gate to their own fastnesses amid the riot of delphiniums and shasta daisies there.

Shall they take the way through the woods? — now no longer bespangled with primroses; they and the dancing daffodils are sleeping until Spring shall call to them again. But the beeches are resplendent in the full glory of their summer sheen. Under the canopy of their branches the brightness of the day is dimmed; its stillness is doubly hushed. There they may linger and, being silver-silent, may hear the faint rustling of the woodland creatures — a squirrel foraging amongst the beech mast and sitting pert afore his tail while he samples his find in tiny paws held to his mouth — a blackbird cracking a snail at his favourite anvil stone and afterwards tossing it time and again in the gritty sand to condition it to his gizzard — a rabbit, perhaps, who fed but lightly at daybreak and ventures out at high noon to make amends; timid and watchful, he is ready to scutter at the least movement and stamp the ground in warning to his brethren in the burrow.

Out beyond the spread of the beeches, a tangle of briar and bracken springs luxuriant from damp mossy banks, each frond and tendril thrusting upwards to the light in its determination to grow to the utmost whilst the day holds warm. And again, close under the silver birches, a magic circle of gaudy coloured toadstools is set haphazard around a verdant oasis of greensward. If, for the nonce, no elfin sprites skip amongst them it can only be that important woodland duties have called them elsewhere. In high summer they must minister to so many tiny creatures that there is no time for relaxation; that must wait until the brief starlit hours of night. Then will owls look down wide-eyed and solemn upon their gambols, whilst flittermice scud overhead in a frolic of their own.

A gravelly track winds down and away to a deeper seclusion. Through half-closed eyes a lithe figure may be glimpsed swinging along it through the brushwood. He is clad in Lincoln green. A quiver of arrows is belted to his back; his bow is slung about his shoulders. He steps lightly in long soft boots of deerskin laced crisscross to the knee. The woods are his world; they provide him with sustenance and shelter, with fuel and clothing. They bring him contentment and peace.

As the road winds onwards and away it must, in that soft country, lead to some old bridge of stone where it narrows and humps itself to span the rivulet beneath. Gracious willows stand close to the bank framing, with their greeny curtain, the spread of water meadows beyond. Surely they will linger here, leaning on the bridge's parapet to daydream an hour away. Who could hurry by? There is fascination in watching the water moving so leisurely at a little distance from the bridge, almost coming to rest where it widens to a pool and then sweeping to the arch in tiny cascades as if in sudden realisation that the one purpose of the day is to scurry through and find what lies between the banks on the other side. All day and every day it gurgles continuously under the bridge. Whence does it come, and whither away?

Down in the clear shallows, shoals of tiny minnows and gudgeons have their haunts where the water runs smoothly. They stay, apparently motionless, head to the current, each one holding his place in the shoal to a hair's breadth. At the splash of a pebble, they dart upstream in a lightning flash only to drift back immediately to their old station — and all without the slightest break in formation. The larger perch rove through the water in line ahead entirely ignoring the presence of such insignificant fry.

Here the swallows fly unceasingly — wondrous feathered creatures whose whole life is spent a-wing. When autumn comes their very survival on the long migration flight to the distant Indies will depend upon what insect food they can now absorb to build their strength. No hour must be wasted in the quest. And then they will return again with unfailing instinct to build their nests with mud from the banks of the rivulet so that when their own fledglings take the wing they may in turn share the plenitude of food.

Today they fly low, for the tiny gnats they pursue have not risen into the upper air. It is a dream of delight to watch them from the parapet flashing back and forth below — now skirting the bank, now skimming the surface of the water so close that oftentimes they flip the crest of a tiny ripple with a butterfly kiss. Time and again one or another will bear down towards the bridge so swiftly as to bring a gasp of dismay in the fear that he will flatten himself against the stonework. But in the last instant he deviates and flashes up and away overhead to circuit the stream again.

The gaze may lift from watching the vivid life in the elements of air and water close under the parapet, to the vista of the water meadows. Shaded to the deepest green where the rivulet courses them through, they lie in a quilted pattern hemstitched by the hedgerows and bedecked with such profusion of colours as only nature dares to mingle — the azure of cornflowers, the red flame of poppies, the gold of cowslips and buttercups.

Truly, the hour spent in contentment here is theirs to recall in all the days that are to come.

Ever the road leads on. It sweeps across the common, its unfenced boundaries an invitation to explore what lies beyond the scattered gorse bushes ablaze with bloom. Geese there are, busy with their browsing, who resent this intrusion upon their rightful preserves and advance menacingly with outstretched necks hissing their displeasure. This is where valour can be carried too far; a tactical retreat is the better course so long as it can be achieved without the appearance of panic. That may easily bring disaster. The more friendly donkeys, however, welcome a respite from the interminable occupation of seeking nourishment at ground level. It is impossible to deny their meek appeal for more enticing food but nonetheless it is a grave mistake to give in. If so little as one crust from the luncheon basket is fed surreptitiously to the more dejected-looking, a telepathy will spread throughout the common. One after the other they plod toward the growing circle and stand mutely as to say "And me — see the burden of sorrow I carry. Is there no small crust for me? Ah lack a-day!"

So much there is of enchantment in the sunlit hours; they glide away unmeasured. Now, as the sun slants to the horizon, the blue of the sky shades through brilliant orange and vermilion to the dusky violet of evening. The warmth of the day subsides. A stillness more profound than the daytime hush steals over the land. Now the time is come for the bicycles to be headed homeward before darkness completely envelops earth and sky.

How exhilarating the ride home through the quiet of early night. From the hedgerows the dogroses pour out their perfume into dew-laden air to form invisible pools of fragrance. Where the trees have shaded the road the air is chill and invigorating. They ride fast and tingle with the nip of it. Where the road dips to a hollow, a mist has formed. They switchback down into the unknown, trusting there is no turn to left or right before they emerge again.

And, upon reaching home, to be met with the glad greeting: "You girls and boys must be hungry. Have you had a good day?" And the answer, with deep satisfaction — "Yes, we have had a lovely day — a glorious day — and please what is for supper?"

These were journeyings of exploration. It was of little consequence where they finished up or when. It was rather a different matter if the intention was to spend a whole day on the coast. If Yarmouth was the objective, the first care must be that you arrived with the toll fare — 1 shilling and $^{1}/_{2}$d. At the entrance to the town was a toll-bar across the road and that sum was demanded before it would be raised to allow a cyclist to pass. The alternative was to turn round and cycle the 20 miles home again. The toll-keeper was allowed no discretion.

For the last ten miles the road led in a beeline across the flat marshes. There was not so much as a bush or tree to offer shelter and the daily change of wind from a sea breeze in the morning to a land breeze at eventide was just the opposite of what was wanted. We knew, too well, the anti-cyclist wind on the Yarmouth road. Moreover, cattle being driven to market from the marshes kicked up the flinty surface so that one or more punctures were almost a certainty. If the puncture was a slow one, the better scheme was to pump the tyre hard and plug along against the insistent wind until the tyre softened again. So you made headway by alternate pumping and plugging, only to find in the end that the puncture was rapidly getting worse and the only course was to strip the tyre and mend it.

However, we, as miller's children, could scarcely justify any complaint against the wind that blew us no good on the road. The same wind was even then blowing us good at home, turning the mill by which we had our being. But that our trials should have been made the worse by meandering cattle of unknown ownership! We sometimes wished that we could be in charge of the toll-gate at the time they went through. The price per head would have been phenomenal.

The University of
the Road

All during the summer the miller went around visiting
the outlying villages to discuss with the farmers the
prospects of the growing crops. On many a summer's
evening, after the work of the day was done, the cob was
harnessed up in the high gig and driven out to a distant
farm. These excursions were a delight to the youngsters.
Two of them would often be taken as well. Upon arrival,
the business between miller and farmer was never
hurried. It might start with both of them leaning at a
five-barred gate, chatting of mutual acquaintances and
local doings. By imperceptible degrees, the subject
would drift to the true purpose of the discourse — how
many quarters of corn would be harvested this year; its
condition; whether it was to be threshed from the stook
at harvest or stacked and threshed later in the year and
(here the shadow-play and finesse was at its height) the
price. By this time, it was more appropriate to carry on
the discussion within doors, seated in the farm kitchen
alongside a large jug of homebrew or farm cider.

Meanwhile, farm children would emerge from various
directions, shy and hesitant. Were these visitor children

of the country or the town? Did they speak the same language? Soon the ice was broken and we were taken around the buildings to see all the baby things, furred and feathered; taken to explore the water meadows down by the stream and across the single-plank bridge to the coppice where water hens nested in the rushes; taken for rides on their favourite pony. The hour slipped by so fast. As twilight deepened we too gravitated to the kitchen to find there monstrous slabs of harvest cake and delicious milk from the cool recesses of the stillroom. And then came the drive home through the night's early dusk — we aglow with contentment and my father cheered as much by farm cider as by the success of his deal in wheat futures.

Each gig lamp shone with the magnificence of one candle power, for they were in fact constructed with a long hollow stem beneath the lamp to contain a tallow candle which was thrust upwards by a flexible spring as it burned away. Not, of course, that any illumination of the road was really needed — the cob knew his way home well enough without it, but the law said so, and even a country policeman could be a little difficult of persuasion if he thought his authority was being flouted.

According to the arrangement made with the farmer, wheat was delivered to the mill at varying periods throughout the year. Just before harvest, the roundhouse and granaries would be empty. Immediately afterwards they began to fill and would reach bursting point, as the threshing engine journeyed round the countryside, calling on one farmer after another to thresh his stacks.

The customer, however, must have flour regularly.

The Sack Hoist

The housewife's flour bin was in keeping with the size of her establishment but, big or small, the situation would become precarious if she had to scrape the bottom of it. She trusted to the miller that she was not placed in that predicament and, in fulfilment of that trust, the mill cart made its round with never-failing regularity. Only on the rarest occasions in winter, when the roads became so snowbound as to be absolutely impassable, would his

29

deliveries be postponed. In such weather, it was the more important that animals as well as men should not go hungry and, as day succeeded day without a break in the weather, the miller became restless and uneasy. He knew those of his people who had failed to lay in a little extra stock and naturally they were amongst the first to be visited when movement was again possible.

By some unexplained custom, the unit of measurement of flour was a "sack" weighing 20 stone, but no miller at that time ever put up a sack of flour. It was not only that people did not purchase flour in that quantity, but it would take the strength of a Samson to lift and handle it. So, flour was put up by the half-sack, and many a domestic flour bin was made to take that amount. A 2-stone bag was however a more usual supply to a country cottager.

From very early days, we youngsters were permitted to accompany the mill cart on its delivery rounds. Being a large family, we had to take our turn as passenger just as we shared so many other things. In this way each one of us came to know the countryside intimately over a radius of many miles. I think the most desirable journey was that to Postwick, some eight miles distant, which lay at the extreme edge of the miller's territory. The promise that we might go was always dependent upon there being room for us after the mill cart had been fully loaded but, invariably, there seemed to be a small niche amongst the sacks which could accommodate one small boy.

It was a long journey for the carthorse and, laden as he was, he could only go at a walking pace until the load was considerably lightened. The way led by Heartsease Lane skirting the Heath to the first points of call amongst the beautiful wooded uplands of Thorpe, and thence down to Thorpe Hamlet itself.

The fascination of Thorpe Hamlet was never ending. The narrow road wound along through the straggling village, bordered by the river Yare on the southern side and by sweeping uplands to the north. The Hamlet had no choice but to accommodate itself to the space between them. It made the most of the opportunity to broaden itself wherever the river receded from the hills. Here rose gardens and meadows stretched to the water's edge. Then it was squeezed up again until the houses abutted on to the road itself so that it had to elbow its way through. It became spacious and lovely where the road ran alongside the narrow village green, itself bordered by gracious chestnut trees next the road and by the river bank on the far side. Thorpe, the one time home of he who painted so gloriously — John Cotman.

Through the Hamlet we threaded our way — to deliver flour to this house down by the river, oats and wholemeal to that one standing back amongst the trees. Cottage kitchen and manor house alike awaited our coming and greeted it with kindly welcome.

And so we were come to "The Griffin" and it was lunch time for man and horse. He knew the routine of the round as well as his master; neither bit nor bridle was required to guide him into the Griffin yard.

First he must be haltered up in the shelter of the stalls and given his nosebag of chaff and oats before we went in to call on the landlord.

31

It would have been inconceivable that any of the youngsters would have been permitted, in ordinary circumstances, to enter a public house. But this was the Griffin — a hostelry of the road — and normal conventions were stood aside.

You felt at first a little subdued as you followed the miller in from the bright sunshine to the cool shady bar parlour. There were never more than half a dozen wayfarers at that time of day — a couple of watermen perhaps, who had brought a wherry 30 miles up the river from Yarmouth, a villager or two, a wagoner fetching brewer's grains from Norwich, and ourselves. Everything was of absorbing interest. You stood, rather overawed, close by the miller as he gave his order for refreshment which you then carried over to the old oak settle by the window whilst he conversed with the landlord. The fare was simple indeed — large square biscuits and an immense wedge of Dutch cheese, to be followed by a big currant bun and all to be washed down with brewed ginger-beer from a Toby mug. Griffin fare in Griffin surroundings went to enhance the excitement of this lovely day.

Surely this must be one of those caravanserai which acts as a clearing house for the gossip of the entire countryside. You heard related the whole activity of the river down to Breydon Water — the cargoes of the wherries, the exploits of lame ducks, the workings of the swing bridges — all the life of the river. How, if your father was a miller, could you achieve the high estate of a wherryman? And would it be taken as a heresy against the family tradition if you voice a determination to do so? But, hold, presently the wagoner tells of his experience over at Blofield — how they finished harvest in record time and held harvest-home in celebration of the feat. There was no harvest-home in a wherryman's life so perhaps, after all, it would be better to become a farmer and grow wheat for the mill. These decisions were so very difficult.

However, our journey lay ahead of us. We must move on to Postwick. A couple of miles from the Griffin we turn from the main road and presently come upon the village in its hiding-place set on the edge of the uplands within a great bend of the river. This is the noontide hour of quietude. The village is somnnolent. So peaceful and undisturbed it is that we seem to be the only link with the world outside. We make our calls as quickly as we can but the housewives relish a friendly gossip and, as part of his business, the miller likes to know the domestic happenings in his territory. He is, moreover, often called upon for his counsel in these matters.

At last the final call is made and, except for some empty sacks, the mill cart is empty. We are ready for the return journey. Seeing that there are no longer any full sacks to sit upon, the seatboard is placed in position across the top of the cart and you perch upon it beside the miller. Only he is the more comfortable because his feet rest on the floor, whereas your own dangle in mid-air and you have to grasp the edge of the seatboard to avoid toppling over backwards.

For part of the way we retrace our steps towards Thorpe but there is no need to traverse again the tortuous road through the hamlet, so we keep to the unfrequented ways and go by Thunder Lane. This time, as we pass the Griffin, the carthorse makes no attempt to enter the yard but, all the same, he acknowledges it as a landmark by cocking an ear in its direction.

A carthorse can walk at a fair pace if he has a load behind him against which he can thrust his shoulders. Without it, his action is impeded and his ambling gait is much slower. On the other hand, his build is too heavy to permit him to trot properly. Between the two, however, he has a useful jog-trot. So, after we have reached the top of the rise in Thunder Lane, the miller gives a flick to the reins and we settle down to that easy pace for the remaining six miles.

The high hedges of the narrow lane interweave with the overhanging branches of the trees to form a leafy mile-long tunnel into which the light can only penetrate indirectly. It is moist and cool after the hot sunshine of the open road, and visions of an African jungle come upon you. What might not be lurking in the depths of the woods on either side? The rabbits that scuttle away from the banks might just as easily be carnivorous creatures of the forest.

At the turning into the Plumstead Road we meet the sun again. The horse tosses his head and gives an equine snort of satisfaction and even quickens his pace momentarily in the knowledge that he is now well on the homeward stretch.

We journey in solitude. Nothing overtakes us for the road is deserted on this slumberous summer afternoon. Presently, the miller hands the reins over in token that you are partner as well as passenger. He is in discursive mood and enthrals you with the lore and logic of the countryside and the exciting happenings of his young day. In farming or millering no problem is too difficult of solution from the seat of the mill cart. It is a veritable university of the road. However, as the afternoon wears on a sleepiness gradually overpowers you. Many an undergraduate has had the same experience. The day has brought such an abundance of pleasure that you are filled with contentment. Even the horse drowses in his stride so that he stumbles and has to be abruptly admonished; and then his clip-e-ty-clop clip-e-ty-clop drones on again as before.

Eventually the desire to sleep becomes completely irresistible. You gather together the empty sacks and improvise a couch on the floor of the cart. As you close your eyes you experience a most curious phenomenon; the motion of the cart appears to go into reverse and, try as you may, you cannot coincide with the direction in which you know you are heading. You fall asleep resigned to the thought that you will awaken once more in Postwick.

When in fact you do awaken, it is with the impression that something disastrous has happened. There is no noise of horse's hooves, no jolting motion and only a subdued light. But you distinctly remember falling asleep in the cart and, indeed, here are the very sacks upon which you lay down. You scramble up expecting to find yourself on the roadside, the sole survivor of a terrible accident. And then the true situation slowly dawns upon you as full consciousness returns. Whilst you slept, the journey home has been completed, the cart has been backed into the shed, the horse unharnessed and led away to the stable, and you have been left to your slumbers.

Well Water

Throughout the village, deep wells were the only source of water supply for drinking purposes, although everyone had soft water butts in which rain water was collected, for there was a hardness in well water which made it less suitable for washing clothes. Besides, rain water descended from above upon the just and unjust alike without the aid of human effort, whereas well water came up from below only with the expenditure of much physical exertion.

The larger houses each had its own well; the smaller ones shared a community well. All told, there must have been over a hundred of them in the village.

Who shall sing the praises of the well-sinker?

If the well is to be sunk to any great depth, it must be at least six feet in diameter in order to provide working space at the bottom of the shaft whilst it is under construction. Also, it must be lined with bricks to prevent the sides from collapsing inwards. This lining, in the well-sinker's language, is called the steining. The resourcefulness of an earlier generation is shown by the method adopted for sinking and steining the well. Obviously the shaft could not be sunk to its full depth before the steining was applied; the walls would collapse in the very early stages. No, the steining must follow so closely on the excavation that at no time is any part of the earthen wall left unprotected. In actual fact, the first course of bricks to be laid at the very beginning of the excavation work finishes up as the lowest course at the bottom of the well. The brickwork followed the well-sinker as he went down. How was it done?

A flat ring of timber, somewhat resembling a large hoop, was prepared upon which the first circular course of bricks was laid. This is the well-sinker's "curb". Its outside diameter was the same as that of the shaft to be sunk and it was built up in segments to a thickness of about four inches. On the underside, it was shod with a circular iron shoe which had a sharp edge at the outer periphery to cut into the soil.

The well was started as a shallow excavation only a few feet deep. In it the curb was set truly level and the first of the steining was built upon it as a low circular wall; no mortar or cement was used. The well-sinker then got inside his walled home where he was henceforth to spend many a long day. He proceeded to dig away the soil at the bottom and scrape it under the curb, causing it to subside with it. His helpers above ground continually added more bricks at the top.

A windlass was rigged at the wellhead to hoist the large buckets into which he shovelled the excavated soil and sent it to the surface to be barrowed away. And so the process went on — down, down, foot by foot, until the water-bearing stratum was reached.

Sometimes the steining would become earthbound — that is to say that the earthen walls of the shaft would swell and grip it, so that it would no longer subside as the soil was scraped from under the curb. At first sight this had the appearance of a major calamity. So much work had been expended without having struck water and now no further progress could be made because the steining would not follow down. The well-sinker's ingenuity was, however, equal to the occasion. The situation was met by starting again, at the depth already reached, using a new curb slightly smaller in diameter than the inside diameter of the old refractory steining. The completed well would bear evidence that the trouble had been encountered since a step would be formed where the larger diameter of the upper steining joined the smaller diameter of the lower. Sometimes two such steps could be seen.

At Sprowston, the water-bearing stratum is deep down; in places, as at the Mill House, one hundred and twenty feet down. This is no ordinary hole in the ground. The well must be sunk truly vertical to this depth. The work is risky and precautions must be taken at every stage to guard against subsidence and accident. Working conditions were rendered the more uncomfortable by the seepage of surface water through the steining, so that the base of the shaft was always wet. Moreover, the stagnant air became heavily charged with carbon dioxide exhaled in the breath. This gas, being heavier than air, tended to stay at the bottom of the shaft instead of mingling freely with the air above. Some relief could be obtained by using pans filled with lime water to absorb it.

The quantity of bricks used for the steining was almost the same as that required for building the house which the well supplied with water. The soil hoisted from the shaft, a bucketful at a time, amounted to something like two hundred tons. Verily, well-sinking was a formidable undertaking. It is amazing to think that so many of them were sunk, but water is the first essential to existence and there could be little hesitation in the matter. There were four of them on the Mill House property alone.

The consternation of the house-builder of today might well be imagined if, when all the plans had been discussed and arranged satisfactorily, the architect were to say — "And now for the well. We shall require the same number of bricks as for the house and the cost of placing them out of sight underground will be about the same as for building the others on the foundations. Shall we double the estimate?"

Water at the bottom of a well, however, will quench nobody's thirst. The more elementary method of bringing it to the surface — the one we usually picture — was to erect at the wellhead a winch, to the drum of which was secured a rope or chain with the bucket attached. In the case of a deep well, it was to much greater advantage to use two buckets so that as one descended the other ascended the length of chain being such that, as the lower bucket struck the water the top one appeared at the wellhead. As the full bucket left the water, the water-drawer had to exert all his effort because the weight of a long length of chain was against him as well as the full bucket. But soon after the buckets had passed one another half way down the well, the weight of the ascending full bucket was more than counteracted by that of the chain attached to the descending empty one and, from then on, it was necessary to steady the motion by a braking action on the wheel of the winch.

Thus was the water won — a bucketful at a time, by the expenditure of much hard work. As may be imagined, after the winning it was not wasted.

One of our neighbours took a great pride in his well. Usually the well was situated in the yard, a little distance from the back door, but his was sunk in a special well-house adjoining the scullery. With a little persuasion he could be induced to set a lighted candle in the bucket and lower it to the surface of the water whilst we youngsters peered down in awe and, certainly, one candle power was never viewed in more striking circumstances. It gave the impression that it was shining from the very bowels of the earth and led to the most advanced theories as to how the water found its way there. One could almost imagine the whole country floating on a huge subterranean lake.

An open well, however, was not the most satisfactory arrangement. There was always the possibility of the water becoming contaminated by bird or beast which might find its way to a watery death. A pump was much better, for then the well could be entirely bricked over, leaving only the pump head projecting from the ground. And of course water could always be obtained on the instant and in a continuous flow by working the pump handle.

To outward appearances, the pump appeared such a simple mechanism, consisting merely of a handle and a spout. So surely as the handle was swung, water gushed out from the spout. The simplicity, however, was all above ground; beneath were all the contrivances for bringing the water to the surface from a depth of 120 feet. Naturally there had to be a pipe leading from the water to the pump head and, before iron pipes were made, a wooden one had to be contrived. The sections of this pipe were called pump trees and they were correctly named, for trees they were. Each section was a log about ten feet long and eighteen inches in diameter, bored throughout its length with a six inch diameter hole. They were socketed one to the other and a dozen of them were required to reach down to the water. They hung supported from a staging built across the well just below the surface of the ground. The actual pumping cylinder of brass was attached to the lowermost tree. In it was the plunger which was worked up and down by means of the pump handle above, to which it was connected by a wooden rod (again assembled in sections) leading down through the central bore hole in the pump trees. This plunger forced the water up through the same bore hole.

The miller's first job each morning at the Mill House was to pump water for his horses and two buckets full for household purposes indoors. Water seemed to be in much the same category as the wind which turned the mill — it was to be had for no cost at all; forgetting, of course, that in bygone years someone had to sink the well just as someone had to build the mill. But, even as sails had to be refitted periodically, so did pump trees require replacement, and in each case the repair bill exploded any idea that wind and water cost nothing.

I love the classic picture of maidens drawing water at the well. The scene is idyllic. They gather in a bevy at the wellhead, not only to fetch water, but to exchange the gossip of the day and preen themselves in the sunshine. Their faces are bright with happiness, their robes sway in the soft breeze. Birds flutter around them in anticipation of a tiny drink from such spillage as occurs when the water is decanted into pitchers. These the girls bear away on hip or shoulder as though they were the lightest gossamer.

And then there comes another picture, of a frail old man at Sprowston who devoted all his time to drawing water single-handed. Day by day, in winter as in summer, in rain as in shine, that was his task, for upon him his womenfolk depended for water wherewith to carry on their laundry. A few years ago he could work more quickly. He had sufficient strength to turn the well wheel by its handle and he could carry two full buckets without staggering and slopping it over. But now his strength is failing. He grasps the wheel at the rim and turns it by moving hand over hand and he can manage to carry no more than half-filled buckets. In a hopeless endeavour to lighten his task, he is inclined to lubricate the wheel spindle too freely so that the oil drips into the water or the feather with which he applies it may even escape from his hand and float down the well. And so, what with a meagre supply of water and its contamination by an oily film, the patience of the laundresses is sorely tried.

The old man served his well to the end. But, if ever Fate was ironical, surely she was with him. It was his destiny to spend the greater part of a lifetime at the arduous work of drawing and carrying water without knowing the blessing of a continuous flow to be had at the turn of a tap. And then, just one week after he had drawn his last bucket and would thirst no more, the water mains were connected to the laundry and the well was sealed over, never to be used again.

North Sea Fishing

The dumpling is indigenous to Norfolk. It is to be confessed that it has never achieved status as a national dish in the same way that Yorkshire pudding has become established as the accepted complement to roast beef. There are doubtless good and sufficient reasons for this, but nonetheless in Norfolk it would be heresy to voice any one of them:

> To dumplings Norfolk men are true
> As Irishmen to Irish stew
> As Highlanders to porridge;
> They eat them ever far and near
> From Sandringham to Horsey Mere
> From Narborogh to Norwich.

But the county does not keep all its dumplings in one saucepan. It may claim to make some small contribution to the dinner table in the form of the condiment — mustard — that goes with the national roast beef; at breakfast its contribution is a much more substantial one:

The dumpling's not the only food
For which, for man's beatitude,
The County's more than noted.
The herring in his millions strong
Arrives at Yarmouth all day long
Imploring to be bloated.

Implore as they may, however, not all the herrings arriving at Yarmouth are converted into Yarmouth bloaters. Some are sent to market in the nude, as it were, to be consumed as fresh herrings. When lightly smoked they are identified as bloaters, when much more heavily smoked and salted they take upon themselves the character of highdrieds or red herrings.

And then there is the kipper. If this is to be his final estate, the herring is first gutted by slitting him down the back and opening him out flat before sending him to the smokehouse, where he is cured in the smoke of a fire fed with oak sawdust.

But, in the philosophy of Mrs Beeton, before he can be cured the herring must be caught. That process in the herring industry is of the utmost simplicity — otherwise the fish could not be accounted for in their millions. A net is used, of course, but in a somewhat unusual manner. More generally a fishing net is used to encompass the catch in a small space from which it cannot escape. In herring fishing all that is necessary is to suspend the net vertically within a few feet of the surface of the water. The herrings are obliging enough to catch themselves.

In the course of long geological ages during which they developed as a species, they must have acquired instincts to protect themselves against many of the dangers surrounding them in their marine habitation; but here is a man-made contrivance of which they have no experience. Consequently, their habit of darting about within the shoal is in nowise interrupted by the presence of a net in their midst. The gills, which were brushed to the closed position as the head entered the mesh, are now opened again and function as barbs to prevent the head being withdrawn. The herring is caught. There he will remain until a sufficient number of his fellows have made the same fatal mistake, upon which the net will be hauled. The limit of the catch is reached, in theory, when every mesh is occupied by a herring's head — a phenomenon which, needless to say, has never been known to occur in the history of the industry.

Herring fishing at Yarmouth was carried out on the grand scale — it still is, although the conditions have changed. The herring boats — known also as smacks or drifters — were then individually owned and every skipper took on his own crew. As his circumstances improved, he might become the owner or part-owner of other vessels to be chartered out to one of his cronies on a profit-sharing understanding.

The enterprise was both speculative and hazardous. Speculative because of the many expenses incurred in outfitting the smack with gear and nets, finding the crew, meeting harbour dues and so forth — all of which, should the season prove unfavourable, might amount to more than the returns. Hazardous by reason of the untellable vagaries of the North Sea, bounteous in the harvest she provides in such abundance, fierce and cruel when the tempest rages over her waters, taking the boats and crew down to a watery grave or running them aground as they attempted to make harbour.

We of the Mill House had a favourite Aunt who lived at Yarmouth — or rather, being a favourite, she was an "Auntie" — and when visiting her there was nothing of more absorbing interest than to go down to the quay to watch the herring boats. For a mile or more they lay against the quay, in places three and four deep. Those which first returned to port took the inside berth; they usually had the lightest catch. Their job of unloading was comparatively easy, the fish being shovelled into basketwork skips and handed out on to the quay. The later arrivals had perforce to take the outside berth.

Quite frequently their delay was caused by an exceptionally good catch, which filled the hold and overflowed on to the deck to the level of the gunnels until there appeared to be no room anywhere on the vessel for one more herring. They came sluggishly to their moorings, alongside the boats nearer to the quay; their bulwarks well down in the water under the heavy tonnage of fish. They could only be unloaded by improvising planks across the bulwarks of the two or three boats lying between themselves and the quay. Along these the skips of herrings were pushed or carried. It always seemed unfair that an inside berth should not be found for boats with so heavy a catch but this, of course, would have been entirely impracticable so densely were the boats packed, stem to stern, along the quay, a veritable forest of masts, spars, booms and gear.

The quay itself presented a truly remarkable sight.

Skips of herrings from the lighter catches were stood in rows of anything up to fifty skips. For the heavier catches there were not nearly enough skips to contain all the fish, so those available were filled with fish and stood down in a hollow square, into which the catch was poured as it was brought ashore. "The herring in his millions strong" was no exaggeration. Not that anyone attempted to count them.

On the quay, every phase of the industry was in full swing. All this assorted company of skippers and crew, auctioneers and buyers, net makers and chandlers were a close knit community, interdependent upon one another. They had worked together through good seasons and bad, and knew one another's every foible. Never did auctioneers harangue their bidders in such telling terms nor get back in such measure as good as they gave. Half a dozen auctions would be in progress within earshot simultaneously, and salty expressions savoured the whole quayside atmosphere. Buyers were giving directions as to the disposal of their purchases; truckers wheeling them away, and railwaymen arranging freight.

In the midst of all the activity of handling today's catch, preparations were going forward to get other vessels to sea again; not all of them, for crews had earned a night's sleep ashore. But the herring fleet lost little idle time in harbour during the height of the season and everywhere boats were being cleaned down, gear overhauled and victuals going aboard in readiness for the next trip.

Did we say the industry was speculative? There were disappointing occasions when a vessel would come in with a superb catch — 50 last or more — her gunnels almost awash under the burden she carried, only to find that so many others had the same good fortune that the market was glutted. Islands of herring stood everywhere along the length of the quay and, try as he might, the auctioneer could not get even one bid. Eventually, they would be trucked away in ten-ton railway trucks for use on the land as manure; by that time, if their fertilising value might be judged by the stench they emitted, they were more than equal to the best farmyard manure that was ever carted from a mature muckheap. Yes, the industry was speculative.

It could only have been these stirring experiences at Yarmouth as a youngster that persuaded me a few years later, at the age of 15 or 16, to make a voyage with the fishermen. We knew people at Lowestoft connected with the trawling industry and a little cajolery was productive of the desired permission for me to join the *Betsy May* as supercargo on her next voyage. There was some hesitation in the matter on the part of my sponsor. He was concerned that I might find the life rough and, quite possibly, be ill all the time. But at the age of 15, whose enthusiasm would waver at such trifles? I had sailed on fresh water on the Broads in all sorts of craft from dinghies to wherries; now the wider spaces of the North Sea called. I think I had visions of spending long days with books, basking in the stern sheets, helping no doubt with the trawl and learning the way of life of a fisherman. Not all of these came to pass.

And so one summer morning I joined the *Betsy May* in Lowestoft Harbour. My reception was not effusive; a passenger on his trawler was something new in the skipper's experience and he evidently meant to await developments; it might turn out that I was a Jonah on his vessel and that a poor catch would result from my presence. Superstition runs strongly with the fishermen and, indeed, I have known a skipper to turn back an hour's sail from oncoming boom instead of merely rising to let it pass beneath them. They are the ones that get away.

Presently the mainsail was hauled and we made way to the harbour mouth and out to the open sea on a course in the direction of the Dogger Bank. At first there was enough of interest in the working of the trawler and the view of Lowestoft from the seaward to enable me (with some effort be it said) to delude myself that the sensation in the pit of the stomach was but a passing discomfort. It would not be denied, however, and soon nothing would avail but that I must lie down. Here, straight away, was the first hardship.

Amidships of the trawler were the living quarters — the cuddy — which was reached by a short ladder through a hatchway from the deck. At the bottom of the ladder was the donkey engine which was kept under steam for the whole of the voyage; the cuddy opened from the tiny stoke hole. It was not more than six feet across with superimposed bunk cavities and store lockers around the sides. Here the crew ate and slept. No description of the cuddy, however, could possibly convey an impression of the fetid admixture of the smell of stale fish, kerosene, smoke and humanity that permeated it. Ill as I felt, I could not stay there so I lay

51

on the hard deck, huddled in a blanket, under the lee of such shelter as I could find.

Three interminable days and nights passed in this fashion, broken only by interludes when that member of the crew who was designated "cook" brought gracious mugs of hot tea. If this were sea-sailing, let it end soon — whether on sea bottom did not much matter.

And then, with dramatic suddenness, I was well again — well and exceedingly hungry. In all my subsequent voyaging on ocean liners, events have followed the same sequence. I know now that for at least the first 48 hours it is best to plan for nothing but sleep; after that the voyage begins and, come foul weather or fine, can hold no further discomfort.

On the *Betsy May* I discovered the next hardship; there was nothing to eat. All the fresh bread and provisions which had been put aboard at Lowestoft had been consumed, as well as a large cake which I had brought from home and had handed over to the cook at a time when I was convinced that food could never again be of any interest. The fare was now stew and dumpling twice a day for the rest of the voyage.

Trawl fishing is necessarily conducted in an entirely different way from drift fishing, since the fish to be caught are flat fish — plaice, sole and halibut — that live on the sea bottom. The trawl somewhat resembles a huge butterfly net in which the round opening has been squashed to a narrow elongated shape; but, whereas in catching a butterfly you cast the net over it, the fish swim into the trawl of their own accord. A timber boom extends along the underside of the long narrow mouth of the net and this is slowly dragged along the seabed, with the tapered net trailing from it. When the boom approaches a fish, he must rise from the bottom to avoid being crushed and, as he attempts to settle back again after the boom has passed, he finds himself inside the trawl and eventually in the "cod end" — the bag which closes the end of the tapered net. No doubt, upon being disturbed, some fish swim against the direction. Herrings in the bulk are reckoned by the "last" or the "cran" — a last being 13,200 herrings, and a cran thirty seven and a half imperial bushels averaging 750 herrings.

In all that featureless expanse of water, how could anyone decide whether the fishing was likely to be good? So far as I was able to find out, the fishermen had three methods at their disposal: they would first be guided by the depth of water and the appearance of the sea bottom. Both of these they found by casting a lead attached to a line knotted at fathom intervals in the ordinary way. The lead was coated with a heavy dollop of fat so that some of the sea bed would stick to it, to be examined when the lead was hauled up. These two things might decide them to cast the trawl, and then the third came into play; if they caught plenty of fish the fishing was good; if not, it wasn't.

Three times in 24 hours the trawl was heaved. At zero hour — midnight — the helmsman on watch went to the cuddy and bestirred the rest of the crew with a rousing "Up trawl. Ye Ho-o-o". Out they tumbled and drew on their long thigh boots for this was a sloppy job. The donkey engine was stoked up and steam turned on to the hoisting winch. When it was warmed up sufficiently, the drag rope was passed around the bollard of the winch and gradually the trawl came up. As the boom came out of the water the crew stood ready to handle it and lash it to the gunnels. The rest of the net was now hanging in the water and had to be hauled inboard; for this operation the crew took station along the vessel's side and — working as a team — reached out over the gunnels, pulling the net in hand over hand until only the cod end remained in the water. This was too heavy to manhandle because of the weight of the fish it contained; a rope was therefore passed from the winch to haul it inboard and deposit it on the deck. Here it was opened by loosening the line to which the extreme end was tied.

Let it not be imagined that all that came out of the cod end was fish. Much of it was "trash" — inedible creatures dredged from the seabed, broken shell and dirt. The good fish were picked out, packed in boxes and placed on ice in the hold; the trash was shovelled overboard.

Whilst the trawl was up we scudded along at a spanking rate which slowed up as the net was lowered until, when it reached bottom, the water merely drifted sluggishly past the vessel's side.

As day succeeded day in the invariable routine, I found I had not foreseen the monotony of life aboard a small vessel. It was relieved to some extent by the fact that I was now fully accepted by the crew as one of themselves; a novice certainly, but one to whom they could explain the intricacies of their calling and so beguile away their own hours of tedium. Most of all, I think, I was fascinated in those small hours of the morning when the midnight catch had been cleaned up and everyone had gone below again to sleep, except myself and the helmsman — the skipper, perhaps, who was taking the middle watch. It was then that the utter loneliness of the sea became so impressive; nothing existed save only the stars set so remote in the bowl of heaven above, and the dark water swirling away so close — so very close — at the vessel's stern. Much of fishermen's lore I learned in those still hours and came to see how salt water must always win them to its service

After ten days our supply of ice was becoming exhausted and the skipper decided that he could stay at sea no longer. The trawl came up for the last time, its final catch disposing conclusively of any suspicion that my presence on board might prove to be a baneful influence. The jib sail was now set as well as the mainsail and the helm put over to bring us on a westerly course for the coast.

I now discovered why I had come on this voyage. The natural philosopher propounds a theory which determines that the height of waves at sea and the distance between adjacent crests must depend upon the depth of the water in the ocean. The strongest wind cannot raise waves any higher than that dictated by the theory, and similarly the distance from crest to crest is governed solely by the depth. In demonstration of that theory, we met such conditions on the homeward run as would gladden the heart of the most exacting theorist.

From early morning we had run before a strong breeze which stiffened as the day wore on until, by noon, it had reached almost gale force. The sea, which had been moderate to begin with, increased with the rising wind and tufts of white horses appearing on the crests of the waves showed that they had reached the maximum height they could ever attain in that water.

From the crest of a wave the outlook showed the sea to be heaving with the most regular series of rollers following endlessly one upon the other; down in the trough nothing was to be seen beyond the two walls of water stretching away on either side of a mighty gulch. We were now running with a following sea, dead across the waves. My position in the stern sheets provided a view of everything that was happening aboard — the big boom of the lug sail well out abeam straining at the blocks; the skipper at the helm watchful of it whilst he continually eased away in the troughs and held to the wind as we rode the crests; a couple of the crew standing by at the foot of the mast.

The length of our little vessel was somewhat less than the sloping side of the waves from crest to trough — a circumstance which provided thrill upon thrill. At one moment she would balance on the crest of a wave in hesitation whether or not to take the plunge down its flank. Having decided to do so she would pitch down at such an angle and with such speed that for several seconds it appeared impossible that she could lift her prow again before the wall of water immediately ahead fell in an avalanche and overwhelmed her.

No sooner had this anxiety passed than the stern would fall away from where it was perched on the wave's crest, pointing to the sky, to wallow in the very depths of the trough, and again its rate of fall would challenge the immutable laws of buoyancy and bring the heart to the mouth. Each time as she recovered from the downward swoop the water went swirling away aft leaving only a few inches of freeboard between its surface and the rail.

And then would come a rogue wave, of whom the sailors say that he sends his minions ahead to lull the mariner to a false sense of security so that he may be taken off his guard and become an easy prey. This time the stern goes down, down — you await the moment when the water will reach its accustomed approach to the rail and will begin to recede — but, Heavens! look! it continues on — the water surges over the rail in a flood; the rogue has achieved his fell design. This is the end; we are lost.

The skipper, however, remains unperturbed — his hand is at the helm; his eye is on the wave ahead in complete disregard of the one that has passed under the keel. Perhaps, after all, the rogue wave is no novelty to him.

All on board were pleasantly excited at the prospect of making Lowestoft Harbour by nightfall. Possibly the skipper, as navigator, did not share this expectation so strongly, for navigation as practised by the fishing fleet is a very inexact science. In its elements the principle is simple enough; having left Lowestoft in a north-easterly direction, the opposite direction — south-westerly — must be taken on the return voyage. This in itself, however, did not take into account the days we had spent on the Dogger Bank drifting or sailing to various points of the compass according to whether the trawl was down or up. In order, therefore, that we should not overshoot the harbour mouth at Lowestoft, a course was set well to the west of south-west to bring us to the coast above Lowestoft. Once having made a landfall, every skipper knew the landmarks of the coast so well he had no difficulty in making port.

Darkness was approaching as we made our own landfall — the Hasboro' Light; we stood towards it — tempting Providence as it seemed to my inexperience — until the sight of the surf breaking upon its treacherous shoals warned that we must go about. From that point our course lay down the coast some twenty-five miles to Lowestoft. Now we were "running in the trough" — along the waves instead of across them — and a heavy roll took the place of the previous pitching. As each successive wave bore us bodily skyward, we ran along its crest for a few moments before it rolled solidly away to starboard and we subsided down its flank to the bottom of the trough. Here all sight of shore lights was lost, since then the mast scarcely topped the level of the crest of the waves. The black waters sloped away upward on either beam and for a little we forged along the interminable gorge between them and then inexorably we were borne up the flank of the oncoming wave.

If any rogue pursued us now he passed beneath the keel unnoticed, for being broadside-on we rode his crest without knowing that it was any higher than that of his fellows.

58

So we sailed on through the night. At dawn we made the harbour mouth and passed between its marker beacons to the tranquil water over which they stood sentinel. Could this now be that same vessel which all the previous day and night had danced the waves, weaving her way over them and swinging her masthead in abandon amongst the stars? Those frolics were for the open sea where there were none to gaze and frown in disparagement. Here, in the Harbour, one must be decorous as becomes a lady in the company of so many other staid folk. If one rolls at all it must be with only the slightest inclination and that performed with calculated deliberation and grace. As for pitching that, of course, is not to be thought of.

In the silent hours of early morning we come to our berth unobserved by the still-sleeping town. The sail is lowered with a creak and rattle of spars which echo down the length of the deserted wharf. The fisher-folk are home again.

Implements of Husbandry

Year by year Nature performs her wondrous miracle — the Miracle of Spring. Those who live out their lives in the Home Country are, I think, inclined to accept its glory as the normal introduction to summer, whilst the memory of we who have succumbed to the wanderlust is apt to become dimmed. We know inwardly that the break of English Spring is a supreme spectacle but, even with that knowledge, upon returning after years abroad we are swept away with its startling vividness. We find ourselves asking — "Was it always so when I knew it year by year?" and the answer is "Yes! but you were so close you missed something of the wonder of it".

The blush of Spring leads so quickly to the full bloom of Summer — Summer with its long, long days that gradually drift to evening and at length merge so gently and reluctantly into night.

It was one summer when I was a young student that some of us discovered a bathing pool in the upper reaches of the river Yare near the railway viaduct at Lakenham.

We swam early in the morning so that we might be back home for breakfast. For myself the arrangement meant getting up soon after five and cycling the four miles through the city, at that hour still and silent and only just beginning to show signs of awakening. It was of course a martyrdom — no less torturous for being self-imposed. The water was so cold that the few minutes it was possible to stay in it scarcely repaid the effort involved. By breakfast time, however, there came the satisfying feeling that you had already made good use of the early part of the day and the fullness of it yet lay ahead.

Our swimming exploits had unexpected results. Week by week the pool shrank ever smaller as the growth of waterweed encroached upon it, until eventually the only possible way of entering the water was by a flat stinging dive from the bank. Our efforts to clear the weeds were entirely fruitless until an old reed-cutter told how it should be done. The equipment required was simple enough, an old scythe blade with a length of rope attached to either end. To cut the weeds, the rope was passed from bank to bank with the scythe blade lying on the bottom in mid-stream. One person worked on either bank. Each gave his rope a short jabbing tug alternately with the other, then a half-step forward and another sharp tug. The cut weeds floated to the surface and were carried downstream until they lodged against those still uncut at the edge of the pool.

Now our swimming was but a pastime. Two miles further downstream a watermill straddled the rivulet and the miller was seriously troubled because the weed was impeding the flow of water to his mill. Hearing that some young enthusiasts had been doing a little weed-cutting up the river, he sent word that he could give us a real job of work in clearing the river. In a further burst of enthusiasm we agreed.

The miller appointed our old reed-cutter to be foreman and clerk of works. The procedure was the same as that we had used at the pool, except that instead of working with one scythe-blade a string of them were fastened together to reach across the bed of the stream from bank to bank. But had we realised how much effort was necessary to tug so many blades through the water as compared with our own, I think we should not have jumped so eagerly at the miller's proposals.

However, a contract is a contract. We set to work at a pace which must have made every weed in the two-mile stretch of water ahead tremble upon its stalk, thinking that it would not see the morrow's morn. Actually they were safe for several weeks. Our reed-cutter steadied us down at his end of the rope and after an hour's gruelling work we were ready enough to believe that his conception of weed-cutting was a good deal superior to our own. A stripling's ardour is no match for a veteran's fortitude in such circumstances.

Possibly in these days of mechanised processes there is some more effective means of clearing a stream of its weeds. My activities in later life have led me away from the profession of weed-cutting and I have had no call to keep myself acquainted with its developments. I remember thinking at the time that the principle of cutting the weeds with an improvised flexible blade moved over the riverbed was an ingenious one. Certainly it was in advance of the scheme for clearing the weeds from the water once they had been cut. They floated down to the watermill and there, for a hundred yards upstream, they gathered as a dense mass on the surface. For days on end, we struggled with long hooked forks lugging them on to the bank. They had become matted together, making it difficult to separate those speared on the fork from the main mass and were heavy with the sodden weight of water. The work of getting them on to the bank was even more strenuous than cutting them from the river bed.

* * *

When applied to its true purpose, however, the scythe takes pride of place as an implement of husbandry. The hoe, simple tool though it be, follows close behind. Ten acres of beet loom up as an enormous tract of territory when beheld from a corner of the field armed only with a hand hoe with which to chop out the superfluous beetlings. Each row appears endless. And the vastness of the undertaking seems to be only slightly moderated if the single hoe is multiplied four or five fold in the hands of that many workers. Such, however, is the task and the countryman does not quail before it. He brings to it a skill that is not readily apparent. That unerring flick of the hoe to left and right ruthlessly decimates the weeds and precisely spaces the tiny beet so that each is left in splendid isolation to grow to maturity unhampered by its fellows. He brings an easy deliberation of movement —

63

a deceptive action — which enables him to work on through the long day where a novice would tire in a couple of hours. As for monotony — who would find monotony in a job of work under the open sky calling for concentration, skill and accuracy, every minute of the time?

The scythe is even more the tool of an artist. Only a skilled reaper can handle it effectively. Its predecessor, the sickle, was almost as elementary an implement as could be imagined, a curved blade with wooden handle attached, with which to cut the stalks of grain, a few at a time, as they were gathered into a bunch in the other hand. The transition from sickle to scythe was simple enough in conception. The blade was lengthened and made less curved and a longer handle was fitted. The result was a vastly more effective tool and one which called for a much superior dexterity in its operation.

A year's planning, a year's work, culminates in the festival of harvest. Early in the year the land is ploughed and harrowed, the good seed scattered and dock and thistle cut out wherever they threaten the young corn. Sun and rain, wind and dew, have succoured the growing corn until now the ears are heavy with swollen grain. They bend away at the top of the stalks, a delight to the eye as they ripple to every breeze that blows over the field.

The same hands that spent long days ploughing and seeding are now to have the satisfaction of harvesting the product of their labours. Those who sow shall reap. But this matter of reaping must be tackled with due ceremony. The harvestmen come unhurriedly, each with his scythe slung over his shoulder. It is as personal to himself as his own pair of boots; he has selected the curved snead to suit exactly his own stature and reach; he has adjusted the grips to balance easily in his hands; he knows the steel of the blade.

With deliberation they make their plans. Their scythes are laid carefully against the hedgerow. Two of them walk along the headland where the rough grass has already been cut. They survey the field from the slight rise there, for a long day lies ahead and they must estimate the work in front of them.

The preliminaries can now begin. Coats are removed, shirt-sleeves rolled, and trouser legs adjusted where bowyangs secure them below the knee. Then the belt is buckled on, carrying the whetstone in a sheath over the hip. This is the point at which harvesting may be said to begin. It starts with the ringing note of the scythe blade as the harvestman plays the whetstone upon it. How easy it looks. He props up the scythe with the end of the snead resting on the ground and holds the curved blade at shoulder height in the left hand. The quick play of the whetstone on either side of the blade is heavy to begin with. It fades away to the lightest caress as the ring of the metal tells that the blade is razor sharp. Each harvestman adds to the harmony bringing up the whole length of his blade to a perfect edge.

So all is ready. He who is to take stroke makes a few trial sweeps on the headland before taking stance at his swathe. A glance behind assures him that the others are waiting to follow and then he swings to his work. As soon as he has advanced a couple of yards, the next in line steps in and then the next and the next until only the backs of five men are to be seen sweeping in echelon down the field.

This task demands the highest skill of any work in the field. The team works in unison. None must slacken or falter else he disrupts all those in the rear and, indeed, may place himself in danger of their advancing scythe. Every sweep adds exactly the same amount of reaped corn to the windrow at the left and leaves the stubble short as evenly as the pile of a carpet. The steady sway of their shoulders might give the impression that little effort is being exerted, but the work requires concentration of mind and muscle. Only by easy movements would they be able to sustain their efforts throughout the long summer's day.

What of the left-handed scythesman? On the village green, a harvestman is permitted the privilege of batting or bowling left-handed and often acquires merit in so doing by reason of the disorganisation he causes in the ranks of the opposing team. (Be it noted that his peculiarity does not call for the use of a left-handed bat or left-handed ball.) There is no opposing team in the harvest field — unless it be a friendly rival over in the next village — and disorganisation amongst the scythesmen would achieve no merit whatever. Consequently, the left-hand scythe has yet to be made. Neither Father Time nor any of the company he has called to himself down the years has ever used one. Just as the plough must inevitably turn the furrow-slice to the right, so must the scythe sweep to the left.

In the harvest field, the first respite of the day comes with time-honoured elevenses. At this hour the women-folk and children take a hand in the proceedings — and a most important one. They establish a base close by the discarded coats and set about uncovering their baskets of food and drink. Harvest cake is especially satisfying when eaten under a shady hedgerow and barley water, cooled by lowering the bottles into the cold water at the bottom of the well, slakes the thirst of a perspiring harvestman as can no other drink.

As though in acknowledgment of the service they give in taking care of the creature comforts of the menfolk, the women have the prerogative of gleaning the field. Before all the standing corn is cut, two or three of the harvestmen lay aside their scythes and start the work of binding the reaped corn into sheaves. They walk along the windrows and with their feet scuffle up sufficient to form a sheaf and at the same time pick up a handful of the straw with which to bind the loose bundle. Then with a quick twist the band is drawn tight and the ends secured — a sheaf is formed. Another stage from standing corn to stack is completed.

Any scattered straws which may be left lying on the ground after the sheaves are bound may be gleaned. And, if the refreshment has been deserving of grateful recognition, who can wonder that the harvesters are not too meticulous in gathering each last straw into the sheaves. The children vie with one another to see who can make the most attractive looking bunches, decorating them with cornflowers and dog roses picked from the hedgerows. By the time their sharp little eyes have roved over the field, not one single stalk of corn will have been left to wither away in vain.

At a later stage, the carting and stacking provide them with additional pleasure. Quite a small child can lead the placid farm horse amongst the stooks whilst the sheaves are pitchforked on to the wagon. There is of course always the expectation, mostly to be gratified, that when the wagon is fully loaded a ride on Buttercup's back to the stockyard will be forthcoming. She, good horse, makes no objection to the added burden.

Glad and happy days were those spent in the harvest field. The festival of harvest was not confined solely to the harvest-home held to celebrate that all was gathered in.

* * *

The fields no longer resound at harvest to the intermittent music of the whetted scythe. The first to supplant that note was the continuous purr of the horse-drawn mower. What a satisfaction to the farmer to see it driven through the standing corn; to watch the stalks being reeled on to the avaricious cutter and laid flat in a long neat ribbon stretching away across the whole length of the field. What an astounding advance. All that remained was to gather the ribbon into sheaves, tie them with their own straw, and stook them ready for carting to the stack. The scythesman was already in course of decline.

Only a few years later the purr of the reaper was intensified when further mechanism was added, enabling it to perform work hitherto left to the hand of man. The corn as it was cut was now swept into the machine itself and presently, when the packing mechanism decided there was sufficient to form a good substantial sheaf, lo and behold an arm sprang out, encircled it with string, tied the knot and passed it to the ejector to be tossed to the ground. The binder had supplanted the mower.

Could human ingenuity go further? It appeared that the mechanisation process as applied to harvesting was complete. Yet the farmer has been deprived of a proportion of his just reward because a little grain was lost in each of the operations of cutting, tying into sheaves, stooking, carting, stacking and subsequent threshing. No human could recover those scattered grains of corn; the farmer could only invite his feathered friends — turkeys and chickens — to glean them from the stubble and so prevent total loss.

Wonderful as it was in its time, therefore, the horse-drawn binder could not hold the field for many years against the tide of mechanisation which was sweeping the century along.

Today the self-propelled combine-harvester drones over the fields from headland to headland. In one

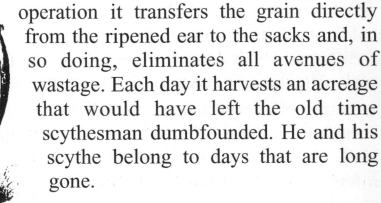

operation it transfers the grain directly from the ripened ear to the sacks and, in so doing, eliminates all avenues of wastage. Each day it harvests an acreage that would have left the old time scythesman dumbfounded. He and his scythe belong to days that are long gone.

As Hard as Flint

The county of Norfolk is not endowed by nature with any outcrop of igneous rock which can be used as material for surfacing the roads. Its clay, marl and chalk, all of sedimentary origin, have determined its character as agricultural country. One material only is available in substitution for natural rock. That material is flint.

The origin of flint is one of geology's most fascinating revelations. It occurs as large irregular nodules embedded in a deposit of chalk. Several distinct layers of them are frequently distributed throughout the chalk bed from top to bottom. In neither composition nor physical properties are they in anywise allied to the chalk in which they are embedded for they are comprised of almost pure silica oxide of silicon — a hard glassy substance, whereas chalk is the carbonate of the metal calcium and is of a crumbly nature.

Now, all chalk deposits were originally formed on the seabed by the accumulation of shells of minute crustacean creatures which swarmed throughout the ocean. At the completion of the life cycle of its inhabitant each tiny shell fell to the bottom of the sea and made a microscopic contribution to the growing deposit. The process continued throughout eons of time until the chalk in some instances reached a thickness of many hundreds of feet. Subsequent movements of the earth's crust, sometimes inexorably slow, sometimes of a catastrophic nature, caused the seabed to rise so that the chalk deposit became dry land.

So far, the sequence of events does not account for the presence of the layers of flint nodules. What agency determined every million years or so that it would be a generous action to add a sprinkling of flints to the seabed so that, when still more millions of years had elapsed and man had evolved, he should discover them and convert them to his use?

The answer is written plain in the record of the rocks. It is abundantly clear that the flint was not formed at the time the chalk was laid down at the bottom of the sea. But, that being so, the still deeper mystery has to be resolved. How came large lumps of flint to be embedded in a thick uniform stratum of chalk, long after it had become dry land?

The solution of that perplexity has also been found. There were other elementary forms of life in the oceans besides the shelly crustaceans. Amongst them were minute sponge-like beings which built up their structure, not from calcium as did the crustaceans, but from silica. Consequently, the resulting chalk bed was impregnated with widely dispersed particles of that substance. Later, under the influence of rain-water, rendered slightly acid in its passage through the chalk, the silica was first dissolved and then redeposited at those centres which developed into nodules of flint.

Far back into pre-history, back in the days of Neolithic man, flint was highly prized for its unique qualities. First, here was a material that could be worked without the aid of tools — if we discount as a tool another piece of flint with which to strike it. Secondly, fragments split from it had a fine sharp edge, making them invaluable as cutting and scraping implements, since from no other source could edged tools come into the hands of these primitive people. Then again, it was plentiful and beyond that, being non-corrosive, possessed a durability superior to that of most modern metallic alloys. To discount these exceptional qualities, it was very brittle.

One is left dumbfounded with amazement in contemplating the determination and resource displayed by Neolithic man in obtaining his supplies of flint. An early "flint mine" is situated at Weeting on the south-west border of Norfolk. The workings date back to about the year 10,000 B.C. and were continued down to 2,000 B.C. During that period, at least 366 shafts were sunk to reach the precious flint, some of them to a depth of 50 feet. The shafts were nearly 30 feet in diameter at the top and some 12 feet across at the bottom where they branched into horizontal tunnels driven along the flint bed. What a prodigious effort! What magnificent assurance on the part of people considered to be not even on the threshold of civilisation! Imagine it; at least 3,000 tons of spoil were involved in the sinking of one such shaft and in number they were equivalent to a whole year of days — and that a leap year. Our amazement is the more profound to learn that the excavating tool was originally nothing more than a piece of bone held in the hand until, in the later excavations, some inventive genius discovered that the antlers of the elk could be broken and used as a crude form of pick, while his shoulder blade became a shovel.

Truly our remote ancestors were a resolute race. The flint, whose winning called forth such immense physical effort and endurance, was indeed almost essential to existence. With the sharp flakes formed from it they would skin the red deer and wild boar and prepare the pelts to serve as clothing. They knew of no garment other than a cloak of skin, so the flint cutters enabled them to clothe themselves against the biting cold. Without it they must go naked.

Nor was it easy to feed from the entire carcase of a deer. But it could be disjointed with the cutters so that all might share the meat. Thousands of years later their descendants devised methods of tipping their spears and arrows with the flint flakes to render them more deadly in the chase. The mining continued and flint-knapping, already a highly developed art, became an organised industry.

The centuries rolled on. The descendants of Neolithic man became civilised. With their discovery of spinning wool and the way to weave cloth, they no longer relied entirely upon the skins of animals for clothing although, even as today, no cloak was more highly prized than one of furred skin. Their edged tools were made of metal instead of the fragile flint. And now their civilisation demanded substantial houses for shelter and these in turn demanded massive enclosure walls for protection against marauders. In flint they found the

73

material for their purpose. The nodules had, of course, to be cemented into the walls and, as though to prove that nothing had been forgotten, a benign Providence had arranged that the same chalk in which the flints were found would make an excellent building mortar. It only had to be heated in a kiln and then puddled with sand and water.

And so the city walls were constructed, somewhat roughly it is true, using the flint nodules just as they came from the chalk beds. No attempt was made to embellish them with features of architectural beauty. Their sole purpose was to provide a staunch rampart against any unwelcome visitor. The dwellers within the city walls, however, strove for a more pleasing appearance in the construction of their dwellings. For this purpose the flints were first broken to expose a smooth glassy surface. Each piece was set into the wall with the smooth face laid to the outside so that when completed the whole surface of the wall was even and shiny in appearance.

But a higher artistry was reserved for the construction of their guildhalls. The good name of the guild was at stake. The builders were on their mettle to show what could be done with such intractable material. Each bit of flint was first knapped into the form of a small cube little more than one inch square and was then set in a mosaic pattern with extreme care and accuracy. Centuries of weathering cannot despoil these façades. They stand impregnable to the worst the elements can bring to bear against them.

74

Then there were the roads. The Icknield Way of the Romans led through these parts. With a colossal expenditure of manpower, they drove their highways mile upon mile connecting outlying encampments with the capital. They realised at that time the need for a staunch foundation and accordingly the road was formed by first laying a bed of large stones — flints — on the prepared surface of the soil. Upon them was laid a covering of gravel and marl to be consolidated by chariot wheels and the tramp of legionaries.

Something better was needed for narrow streets in the towns, some surface which would not give rise to dust and mud. To what else could the townsfolk turn but flint? When laid in the form of cobblestones, it gave a roadway that was washed clean by every shower of rain and was quite adequate for the traffic of the times.

And so we come to the turn of the present century. Only the researches of archaeology reveal that flint was ever won by mining for it. Only the faintest echo of bow-and-arrow days comes to us in the enthusiasm of the modern archer and, even so, his slender shafts are flighted without the aid of any stone. Natural flint can no longer compete with man-made bricks in the construction of dwelling houses. City walls are a relic of the past, and modern progress has outdistanced the cobbled pavement. Are then the usages of flint exhausted? Not entirely!

Along the highways and byways we come upon the old stone-cracker who lives for flint alone. His flints come from the chalk quarries where, as they become exposed in the excavating work, the lime burners set

75

them aside for road making. They are carted away and piled in heaps along the verge of the highway at intervals of some fifty yards, in readiness for the stone-cracker. Every day he works at them and breaks the large nodules into road metal. His art is not on the same high plane as that of the flint-knapper who of yore could knap them into tiny cubes all identical in size. That art is lost forever.

He trudges solitary and placid down the road. Each morning he must travel a little further past the heaps of broken stone and each evening fewer unbroken heaps lie ahead but his task is never-ending for, by the time the last heap is finished, another trail of fresh nodules has been laid for him in a new direction and he must start all over again. He is, of course, known to every user of the highway. Except perhaps for the driver of Her Majesty's Mail van, which may on no account carry a passenger, all are ready to give him a lift on his way.

He does some minor road repairs himself, filling in the worst potholes with broken flint and a shovelful of marl. His cure is worse than the original complaint until the horses' hooves have kicked away the surplus stone and consolidated the remainder.

When the potholes become too numerous the road must be resurfaced. Now comes the steamroller. Here is mechanisation on the roads — as yet the only self-propelled vehicle of any description. What a source of wonderment to the youngsters! What excitement to watch it at work! Its shining cranks and rods endeavour to race ahead of the puffs of steam coming from the chimney but the faster they whirl the faster comes the steam. The eye cannot follow their intricate motion. At a touch of a driver's lever, they slow and come to a stop only to begin their gyrations immediately in the opposite direction, urged to a frenzy by the puffing steam.

A little to the rear, the road-makers fill their barrows with broken flint from the heaps left by the stone cracker. They spread it over the road and others cover it with a dressing of marl. The horse-drawn watercart sprinkles it with water in readiness for consolidation by the steamroller. Some twenty paces ahead walks a man carrying a red flag as the law demands. A curious enactment that! It does not require that as the steamroller goes back and forth over its workings, he shall take station ahead of the direction of motion. No; the law merely says "ahead" and there he stays. When the steamroller advances he moves forward; when it retreats he follows it. The law is oblivious of the fact that only half the steamroller's life is spent in going forward and, so, the rear is left unguarded.

It can scarcely be said that any grave danger arises from this omission. His red warning signal is no larger than a pocket handkerchief. Who would be heedful of it when so close at hand there is puffing of steam and crunching of stone to absorb the attention?

Of a certainty, as a farm wagon approaches, the horses have no thought for him. They look beyond, to this outrageous contrivance which has intruded itself upon their peaceful road. They are of an equine generation which has never known the sight and sound of machinery and they display their disapproval unmistakably. It is of little avail that the steamroller suspends operations to allow them to pass. They stop in their tracks with heads thrown back and nostrils dilated and refuse to draw near to the fuming monster. Only when the road-menders take each of them by the bridle and lead him will they endure such affront and, even so, they prance and perform, never taking their eyes off the offending machine.

This form of road construction was well enough to withstand the wear of ironshod wheels and horses' hooves. A few years later, when the rubber-tyred motor vehicle began to take possession of the roads, it became hopeless. The suction of the tyres removed the binding of marl from the surface and worked it up into the finest flour until it lay upon the road a quivering blanket, an inch or more in thickness. Motor vehicles left in their wake a choking cloud of dust which blotted out visibility beyond a yard's range.

Pedestrians were asphyxiated; their clothes were despoiled. The cloud settled back over the hedgerows and gardens in a dull grey shroud. The situation was unbearable. Some alleviation came from tarring the road surface but its effect was impermanent and the limited supply of tar permitted only the more important stretches of road to be treated. The problem appeared to be impossible of solution. There would never be enough tar to dress all the roads in the country, and how could the cost of treatment be met? It remained for a succeeding generation to find the complete solution in the use of a less fragile rock than flint as road metal, of bitumen as a binding agent, and the motor tax as a source of finance.

This dust nuisance was unknown to the earliest cyclist. He shared the roads only with horse-drawn traffic. Yet he enjoyed anything but perfect freedom from trouble. The flints played havoc with his tyres so that an outfit for the repair of punctures, and spanners for removing the tyres, were first essentials for a journey of any length. Tiny splinters crushed from the road metal had the same razor sharp edge that was such a joy to Neolithic man. To the cyclist they were an affliction to be borne — not always in silence. Woe to the sea urchins!

Millering

The mill stood to the eastward at the top of the garden, showing high above the apple trees. In daytime it swung lazily or turned in full action, according as the breeze blew light or strong. In the evening the sails were stilled, trimmed always to an exact forty-five degree angle as the miller insisted.

From earliest times there were no restrictions to the youngsters playing in the granaries or the roundhouse of the mill, girls and boys alike. Empty sacks made the most wonderful gypsy tents. Amidst the dim recesses of the stacked corn-sacks you could explore uncharted caverns. The entire roundhouse could be converted into a fort to be defended through the grilled openings in the roof against all comers.

Soldier or gypsy, pirate or explorer, all were prone to tumble a few sacks of corn from the stacks. Yet such mishaps were never made the occasion for more than friendly admonition. After all, the up-ending of a few sacks was all in the routine working of the mill. Spillage of corn was regarded rather more seriously. No one was happy about that. We scooped it up to the last grain and tied the sack as best we could. By and large, we were encouraged to regard the mill as something in which we

had a lively share, an attitude which surely returned dividends when the help we could give was of real value.

It was but a small stage from playing on the mill steps to finding one's way into the mill proper above the roundhouse. From earliest days it held a fascination which was unfading down the years. Here was sight of wheels a-whirring, of governor balls flying wide, of wheat trickling to its predestined fate, of leather belts lashing their pulleys around, of oaken beams and quaint contrivings. Here was sound of millstones purring, of the damsel urging wheat to the eye of the runner stone, of the sack hoist's rattle, of the swish of the wind in the sails. Here was felt the sway of the mill underfoot as she rocked in the strong wind.

Still greater the enchantment when a pair of millstones were opened up to be dressed. All their appurtenances

81

had to be stripped away — the vat, the horse, the damsel, shoe and mace — until they stood naked, the heavy runner-stone resting on the nether bed-stone.

Then came the delicate operation of lifting the runner away and turning it on to its back — the exciting phase of the work. Ropes, pulley-blocks and slings had to be drawn from their stowages and made ready.

First, the miller took a crowbar to prize the runner away from the bed-stone — not of course by jabbing it between the two since this would cause a blemish to the surfaces and was to be scrupulously avoided throughout the whole operation. The bite was taken therefore on the iron bands which surrounded the stones and bound together the segments comprising them. As soon as a slight gap appeared, the toe of a large wooden wedge was inserted. By degrees, the gap was widened until a rope sling could be pushed right to the centre of the runner and brought up through the central hole — the eye of the millstone. It was nicely adjusted at the rim of the stone, the pulley blocks were hooked on, and all was ready to take the lift.

Although the pulley-blocks gave a good purchase, a strong man could only just manage to hoist the stone single handed. Even a boy's small effort was helpful. Slowly, very slowly, the gap increased until the stone was standing almost upright on its edge. From that position it had to be overbalanced before the lowering could begin.

To the youngster this appeared a most critical performance. A penny stood on edge between the fingers may be made to lean from one side to the other by the slightest touch. In like manner, the runner had to be thrust beyond the vertical whilst still in the constraint of the slings. A mighty heave of the shoulder was needed whilst paying out a little rope at the blocks. Once having got it leaning over backwards, it could be readily lowered away until it rested snugly on half-filled bran sacks laid on the floor.

In the course of grinding a thousand bushels or so of wheat, the stones became dulled; they dragged at their work and the meal came away sluggishly. A pattern of lands and furrows radiated out from the centre of the stone — the lands being the higher ridges which broke up the wheat berry and ground it to the finest meal, and the furrows the lower valleys by which the meal passed to the rim of the stones to be exuded into the surrounding wooden cabinet — the vat. A small paddle attached to the runner stone swept the meal from the vat into a chute leading to the meal bin on the floor below. When a pair of blunted stones was opened up, the lands presented a highly glazed appearance and in that state the wheat was mangled rather than ground.

The dressing process consisted of cutting fine grooves known as drills in the face of the lands. Meticulous care was necessary throughout. The stone was so hard that it had to be struck a dozen or more blows with the dressing tool — the mill-bill — to cut one small bit of drill. Each blow had to be accurately placed; otherwise, instead of having the surface presenting a neat pattern of drills spaced an eighth of an inch apart, it would be badly mutilated. Stone dressing was the work of a skilled craftsman.

The miller ensconced himself in a half-prone position on the millstone, his elbows well pillowed on bags of bran. He put on his spectacles for protection against the flying sparks and then selected a newly ground mill-bill. This he inserted in its holder, the stock, gave it a sharp click on the edge of the millstone to secure the mill-bill and then set to work. You, yourself, would also get comfortably seated, amongst bran-sack pillows, to enable you to watch more closely.

A few sighting shots in the furrow where accuracy was not called for and the dressing of the lands began. The strokes rang out hard and true, a dozen or more in succession. Then a slight pause as he passed to the next length of drill or a longer one at intervals to hitch up and get more comfortable.

You counted the strokes. Would this bit take more than the last? You made up rhymes and tried to fit the words to the strokes. What would happen when he came to that tiny blemish in the stone? Had he forgotten that part near the eye? Could you catch a spark with your hand? Would it hurt if you could?

Presently, the mill-bill became blunted and had to be changed. You had one in readiness and felt disappointed if he selected a heavier one or a lighter. But the miller's patience outlasted your own. He would have to go on for days before he had finished. The entire surface of both stones had to be worked over and brought up flat and true, checking constantly with the wood-proof.

Close at hand another pair of stones stood idle, but a third pair was hard at work using up the wind whilst the first was being dressed. You watched the wheat trickle from the hopper to the shoe. Its existence as individual grains was measured in seconds then. The shoe sloped down to the millstone's eye and the duty of the damsel was to shake it continuously so that the grains flowed down the slope and disappeared into the eye to the fate awaiting them there. The tempo of the damsel's song rose and fell with gusts in the wind. Nevertheless, she was inexorable in enticing the wheat along; had she failed but a little the stones would run dry and the work of dressing them would be ruined.

At the head of the mill the sails glided silently past the windows, a metronome punctuating the music of the millstones inside. Those windows were of clear glass but, at the side of the mill, they were glazed with bullseye panes, irresistible even to casual visitors as a peep-show which made grotesque figures of objects down by the mill house.

Cog by cog, the windwheel mated with the wallower. It had its place on the topmost floor close behind the sails but, of course, inside the mill. Its immense rim reached down below the horizon of the top floor to mesh with the much smaller wallower in the ceiling of the floor below. Almost silently they turned together, the wooden cogs of the windwheel bearing on the wallower's iron teeth. They were bevel gears, contrived to send the drive from the sails down the mill by the wallower's vertical shaft. Mounted on this shaft, and again in the ceiling of the next lower floor, was the great spur gear which turned the small pinion situated immediately below the millstones. Its spindle passed up through the centre of the stationary bed-stone to the eye of the runner, where it engaged the driving member and so spun the runner around. At length, the force of the wind on the sails had been brought with the power of twenty horses, to the point at which wheat was to be ground.

More there was to fascinate. Millstones had governors. Not to control how fast they should run — only the strength of the wind could turn the sails more quickly — but to ensure that whether much wheat or little ran into the eye it should all be ground to the same fineness. When there came a gust of wind which caused the sails to turn faster, the damsel shook more wheat to the eye. At the same time the governor balls flew wider and thereby permitted the runner to close, by ever so minute a fraction, on to the bed stone.

Yet the wind was harnessed even as it forced the sails around. For if it blew too strongly all the shutters on all four sails would open slightly and spill the wind. This was contrived inside the mill by a weight hanging in the loop of a chain. On a gusty day, therefore, there was within the mill a harmony of all the elements. The wind began to blow a gust, the weight began to open the shutters, the shutters began to spill the wind, the damsel began to hurry the grain, and the governor began to close the stones. Probably, down in the roundhouse, the cat began to kill the rat — or rather mouse, for no rats were permitted sanctuary in the mill. Even the mice did not overstay the cats' pleasure.

Most delightful of all was the top floor. Except where the windwheel drove the sack-hoist, it was devoid of machinery. Nearly all the floor space was occupied by huge grain bins which received the grain hoisted in sacks from the roundhouse. Murmuring noises came from the body of the mill below. Over against the head, the windwheel cogs rose out of the floor in regular succession, swept full circle nearly to the roof and set behind the sack-hoist idler. Their pace was in unison with the wing of the unseen sails outside. Overhead, the roof arched low almost to the touch. Nothing but blue sky was visible from the one wicket at the tail. This of all places was where to come for quiet cogitation upon life's early problems. Solitude was here high above the earth but with sufficient movement at hand that it could never become oppressive.

But, best of all, you clambered across the bins to the wicket window and leant head and shoulders through the opening. The sails were screened from view by the bulk of the mill but just below, built high at the tail of the mill, was the fantail. This was a small circular mill in itself whose duty it was to keep guard over the main sails and hold them always in the wind's eye. It was the benign genie of the mill, a slave, moreover, to the vagaries of the wind. It was a thing alive, whose movements were unpredictable. Let the wind veer but a fraction and it was instantly on the alert, commencing to turn the body of the mill to the new direction.

On a gusty day it was harassed beyond measure. It started to spin this way — hesitated — moved on — turned back, hesitated again. Did the wind intend to veer or was it a false alarm? But no! — the gust was now distinct and strong from the side. It spun away with excited energy. Not for a moment must control be lost.

And then the wind decided to swing back in the first direction and beyond a mean and lowly mockery. But the fantail made no demur. Back it spun, with increased vigour, as though to make amends for the wild-goose chase it had just been led upon. And so throughout the livelong day, and throughout the night as well, when the sails were at rest. For the miller, upon coming to start up in the morning, must never find his mill cross-wise-on to the wind.

The weathervane, too, set upon his mast over the granaries at a little distance from the mill, could be seen searching the wind's direction. He, little spratling, could pick up any deviation on the instant, seeing that he pierced the wind with an arrow-head and had nothing more bulky to move than his own tin shaft and fletches. The fantail, conscious of its burden of responsibility, treated his dithering with disdain. Watching as between the two you could not but feel that, more sprightly though he may have been, the sails were safe in the fantail's keeping.

And so the gaze lifted to the prospect spread afar. From this eyrie, the whole countryside for miles lay open to survey. Close at hand lay Shipfields and the top end of the village. From there, across the line of vision, Mousehold Lane led eastward to Round Tree Corner and beyond to Heartsease Lane, dipping out of sight to the river at Thorpe. The Wroxham and Salhouse roads disappeared northward between coppice and wood into the misty distance. To the right lay Mousehold, its folds ablaze with yellow gorse; to the left Catton, amidst a glory of beeches skirting the deer park.

The landscape lay somnolent under the open sky. Only here and there some faint movement showed that it was occupied by human kind — a Lilliputian race, dwarfed against the wide expanse of field and fallow, a wagon creeping snail-pace to the city, a fore-shortened figure or two moving leisurely through the village, a gardener bending to his plot nearby. Such fantasies as dreams are made of came up to enhance the reverie at the window.

Such attraction was to be had within the mill at all times. Periodically, however, it was increased tenfold. Over a number of years the wind came almost free of any considerable drain on the miller's purse. Yet with it came storm, rain and snow which built up a steadily growing overdraft that had eventually to be met by the re-fitting of sails or other repairs beyond the miller's capability, expert though he was at many a lesser task.

The millwrights had then to be called in, craftsmen who had been bred to the care of windmills through many generations, who knew the peculiarities of every mill in three counties. They were not to be found amongst the engineering firms of the city, not in the county itself even. They came from a small country town twenty-five miles away over the border. We youngsters first knew that anything unusual was afoot when the master-millwright was seen clambering over the sails with my father, prodding the stock (the backbone of the sails), tapping it and taking measurements.

Some weeks later an enormous baulk of pitch-pine timber was delivered to the mill hill. Curiosity grew to excitement when we learned that the sails were to be stripped and replaced with a new set. How would they go about it? How could we help?

When they came — four or five of them — they brought ropes and tackle, saws and sledges. They brought crowbars and enormous wrenches. They were friendly folk, after the manner of sailors. Indeed, their

work of harnessing the wind was somewhat akin to a sailor's. They climbed the "rigging". They used the same knotted ropes. They heaved and hoisted. They set the sails.

Our make-believe at play in the roundhouse now seemed more realistic. Pirates, of course, had always to be driven from our fastnesses at whatever cost. But here were worthy seamen from afar, claiming hospitality, who in return for shelter under its roof and a bed of sacks in the roundhouse would do much-needed work on the mill above, before they travelled on; who, in gratitude for benefits received, would instruct us in the windmill lore of other regions; who, of their friendliness, would teach us the intricacies of hitches and half-hitches, of bights and bowlines; who made the aroma of kippers cooking over an open fire on the mill-hill a joy for ever.

If my father could not get this same perspective of the millwrights' activities it must have been that for him the telescope was turned end for end, or perhaps it was trained beyond the roundhouse on to the job of work on the sails above. And no doubt this enterprise, so thrilling to ourselves, must have brought to his mind matters which troubled us not at all — the cost of "free" wind.

Top Meadow

There should of course be a Top Meadow in any family the size of ours. Its purposes changed as boys and girls grew from toddlers to adults, but always there was abiding interest in the Top Meadow.

It was there in early days that they were taken to sit on a sunny bank, to topple down its slopes, to make daisy chains and blow the time on dandelion heads and, between whiles, hunt in the picnic basket for honey sandwiches and kitchen shortcake. There, later on, they collected hedge clippings and any other combustibles that could be found for the immense annual bonfire. It was fun in the early darkness of a chill November evening to be swallowed up by waves of swirling smoke, to make the fire crackle and flare by stirring it with a long pole so that the sparks flew in showers into the blackness of the night, to roast quantities of potatoes in the ashes when the flames subsided. Bonfire night was an excitement that everyone around looked forward to for weeks ahead.

The meadow lay the whole length of the garden and the width of the mill hill from the house so we were never in danger of disturbing those indoors with our more noisy games. On Sunday, it belonged to the horses. My father believed in turning them out to graze and frolic as the mood should take them and to become refreshed after a week's work on the hard roads in the mill carts. Each one knew well enough what was impending when a halter was placed about his ears instead of the heavier cart-harness and a small boy was hoisted to his back at the stable door. He would begin to frisk even then so that you had to cling tightly to his mane as he was led up the lane and across the mill hill. At the meadow gate you dismounted to sit straddle-legged on the top bar whilst he was released inside.

His antics then were an entertainment in themselves. It was so ridiculous for a heavy carthorse to fling heels and haunches high in the air and charge madly across the meadow as though he were an irresponsible young foal. In his exuberance at finding the soft turf under him he entirely forgot that he was a staid old carthorse. Snorting loudly, he would rush back to the gate with such recklessness that seemingly nothing could prevent him charging clean through, to leave you picking yourself from amongst the splinters. Often he would have to slide on his haunches to avoid striking it. Tiring of this, he next got down on the grass to roll on to his back and flail the air with all four legs, meanwhile wriggling his spine to the ground in an ecstasy of abandon. A few more lusty snorts when he was on his feet again would be the signal that frivolities were at an end and that more serious business must be taken in hand — that of cropping as much grass as possible in the available time.

The horses might also be turned into the Top Meadow on long summer evenings, but there was ample room for our activities without disconcerting them. Our games were largely improvised and that, I think, came about because there were so many of us and our activities were so varied that the funds could not be found to provide proper equipment for them all.

There was the game of tip-cat in which not even a ball was required. It may yet be played in the country but probably more conventional games have displaced it. The "cat" was merely a round hawthorn stick — half as thick as the wrist and about eight inches long — whittled to a blunt point at each end. Another hawthorn stick, about three feet long, did duty as a bat. Let it not be thought, however, that any bit of stick was as good as another; a bat, of a weight and balance which just suited the owner became one of his prized possessions.

Sides having been drawn, the order of innings had to be decided. Since it was most improbable that anyone was in possession of a coin for calling the toss, the invariable practice was for each leader in succession to make one strike. Naturally, the choice of innings lay with that leader who made the longest drive for his strike.

Only at the home base was it permitted to set up the cat. Elsewhere the natural lay had to be accepted. Setting-up consisted of tossing the cat to the ground and tilting it slightly upward by stamping down the rear end. In taking strike, the player hit the forward pointed end, causing the cat to rise with a spinning motion. He had then to be ready to drive it forward with a terrific whack

— not an easy stroke to perform with a round stick upon another one spinning in mid-air.

There is indeed a fine art in that first stroke of tipping the cat. For, if the strike is made too heavily, the cat leaps upward and forward beyond reach so that the succeeding drive stroke cuts only the air or, at best, is not delivered in its full strength upon the cat. And, conversely, if the tipping stroke is too weak the cat will not rise sufficiently and then a full powered drive cannot be brought to bear upon it.

In the course of play, each player is entitled to three strikes in succession. A staunch stroke will drive the cat forward 30 yards or more but, in the uncertainty of the game, the next two strokes may increase the distance only a fraction. Now comes the tense moment for partners and opponents alike. How many runs will he take for his lay? He stands at his end point looking back toward the home base. How many dare he claim? If he is unenterprising and calls too few, his own side will suffer the loss of a proportion of good runs which have actually been struck and then not claimed. But the alternative is far worse. For, if he is too grasping, his opponents are entitled to take up the challenge; that is to say, they may elect to leap the distance back to base in a series of running leaps. If any one of the opposing side can better the call of runs with his leaps, they are added to the score of his side — to the great chagrin of the striker and that of all his partners. He may, of course, "play safe" and nominate so few runs for his strike that his opponents have no hope of leaping them and will not even make the attempt. An outcry goes up then for another fifteen — another ten — another five — to make a game of it.

From the hedgerows came the simple equipment — no more than two sticks — for a pastime calling for dexterity, energy and judgement and providing, withal, a splendid competitive game.

Top Meadow cricket was a game to itself. Certainly, it was much in advance of the backyard variety for we used real stumps for a wicket and possessed one spring-handled bat, somewhat damaged in the blade, as well as others which were not sprung. There were times, even, when we came into possession of a brand new leather ball which lent almost professional status to the game until it burst at the seams or was hit for a lost-ball in the long grass. Then we would be compelled to fall back on the hard composition one whose youthful spherical properties had long since departed. It was the pitch itself, however, which enhanced the uncertainties of the game so much. The only suitable place in the whole meadow had a slope of perhaps one in twenty between wickets. The bowler always claimed privilege of bowling down the slope which meant that the batsman's drives were slowed even before they reached the long grass in the out-field. As though that were not handicap enough, he had a high grass bank forty yards to the off and another low rolling bank to the on-side. Scores were moderate.

The muster of players rarely exceeded three or four a side which meant, of course, that everyone must field no matter who was batting. To drop a catch from one of your own batsmen was deplorable; to hold it was a sublime devotion to the spirit of the game. Sometimes my Father would stroll up to watch the play. Before very long we would have him at the wicket and then the game would become uproarious. On that wicket he was in the same class as ourselves and had no better chance of survival. Efforts to get him out were redoubled in all directions.

The annals of cricket do not record that any one of our company ever scintillated in later years amongst the illustrious players at Lord's. By the same token, no Lord's player ever joined us on the Top Meadow. Had he done so, our pitch and our rules would have introduced him to a game he would scarcely have recognised. He would be dismissed for half-a-dozen reasons that he had never heard of in big cricket.

* * *

It would be impossible to say across the intervening years which of us conceived the mercenary idea of raising revenue.

We were mostly in the red where pocket money was concerned since the return from rabbits and pigeons was precarious and, besides, the effort of feeding and cleaning them had to be sustained so persistently.

The Top Meadow scheme was a venture into the realms of high finance. It could have originated from a most extraordinary crop of mushrooms — several bushels of them which sprang up one year in the far corner. There were always a few scattered over the meadow, but never before had they appeared in such quantity — and they never did again. Very well then, why not raise a crop which was not so erratic and which could be marketed at a profit?

The first year it would have to be potatoes because they "cleaned the ground". But should we be able to sell them? Now that was a defeatist question! This was to be no miniature affair of disposing of a basketful here and there. There would be half a ton of potatoes — perhaps nearly a ton. Think of that! We should have to sell them wholesale. Lots of people would buy half a ton of potatoes — wholesale!

Then again, would Father agree — after all it was his meadow. Not, of course, that we wanted the whole of it, for then where would the horses graze? But our ideas had not carried beyond a certain strip which could be easily fenced off. At first, he said the whole thing was preposterous. How could we dig that matted sod which had been in grass always? Oh! but we were not intending to dig it; we knew where we could borrow a single-furrow plough. And then, of course, we should need the loan of Taffy, the carthorse, to pull it. Please! we could do it all ourselves and not bother Osborne or Smith in the least.

Consent did not come readily. We had to work on the problem, enlarging on this aspect or that, at judicious moments. In the end, he came with us entirely; not, I believe, that we wore him down, but rather it was the habit of his generation to ponder over its decisions. There must be no suggestion of being bustled.

The plough, when we got it, was of an elementary type; its share was very much rusted — a condition we set about at once to rectify by rubbing it down with a half-brick, for obviously such important work as ours could only be done if the tools were in first-class order. We had an oilcan in readiness too, but there appeared to be no place where oil could be applied to advantage so it was not brought into use.

Like every good plough, this one was drawn through the medium of a swingle-tree to which the traces were attached. Taffy's cart-harness was too short in the traces. We had to improvise lengths of chain on either side to place him at a comfortable distance ahead of the plough.

Now, the ploughing could begin. Taffy was suspicious from the outset. Harness he knew, but not harness with chains dangling from it. The Top Meadow he knew but only as a place of unrestricted freedom. We were not to think him so simple that soothing words and a patted neck made up for the indignities we were putting upon him. Where was Smith, who always looked after him; who always treated him as one intelligent being to another; who made satisfying shushing noises as he rubbed down his back and legs; who said "Get over, you old stupid" in such affectionate tones when he nuzzled him in the ribs, bringing chaff and oats to the manger. It was well enough for the boys to be around when Smith was stabling him down — perhaps helping him a bit — but to be taken in charge by them alone was something different. Smith should be there!

A good deal of persuasion was necessary to induce him to back up to the squat thing on the ground that possessed neither shafts nor wheels. He wanted to keep it in view all the time, whereas we wanted his haunches next the plough and not his head. By the time he was hitched up he was in a confused state of nerves. At the first attempt, he took off towards the opposite corner of the meadow at a high rate of knots with the plough-share merely skidding along behind over the thick turf. Evidently our technique was wrong. The share must first be sunk into the ground to the proper depth by digging with a spade. Having done this, so strong was Taffy's determination that, in his next attempt, he almost pulled the whole thing underground and buried it out of sight. No!, this was not the placid art of ploughing as we had seen it in the farmers' fields. There, the furrow-slice turns smooth and even as a ribbon from the advancing share; the ploughman but rests his hands on the handles; the horses forge steadily along with even beat of hooves and heads swinging low. With the open furrow to guide them, they deviate not a fraction from their track. At the headland, a word from their master carries them right to the boundary hedge before they swing to the off. So the stubble is turned, strip by narrow strip, until broad acres lie ready for the seed that shall yield an hundredfold return.

Our own efforts ended ignominiously. Taffy went back to his stable in a state of profound disgust. The plough went back to its owner who must have had a better use for it than we had. The meadow went back to its undisturbed state of thick matted sod. And the boys went back to the meagre but more certain profits to be made from rabbits and pigeons.

* * *

The cricket pitch served well enough for some years but as we advanced into our teens it began to lose its attraction. We were growing up and should be finding our recreation in something more than improvised games. And still the resources of the Top Meadow were not exhausted. One corner of it — not the potato patch but the part that lay beyond the circular boundary hedge to the mill hill — was fairly level although it sloped slightly away from the hedge. Could this possibly be converted into a tennis court? When the idea was first broached early one summer, both my Mother and Father displayed an interest in it that was totally unexpected and most encouraging. This, they saw, would provide recreation for the whole family — girls and boys and grown-ups and their friends besides. Yes! — a tennis court would undoubtedly be an acquisition.

An inspection had to be made at once and never was inspection carried out with greater enthusiasm. See how those bad patches could be re-turfed with sod from another part of the meadow; how easy it would be to build up the ground where it fell away rather sharply. There would certainly remain a very gradual slope from end to end of the court but everybody would have to get used to that — in any event it would give more point to the convention of changing ends in the middle of a set.

The project was beyond the capability of boy labour. Osborne and Smith were called in for evening work to dig post holes for the fencing; to trim back the overgrowing hedges and barrow soil for filling, but they never lacked an audience of small helpers anxious to push, pull and carry. And everyone took turns as groundsman — mowing and rolling the turf and watering the newly laid sod.

It was at about this stage that Neddy, the donkey, made the tactical mistake of betraying too great an interest in what was going on in his meadow. Friendly little moke that he was, he could scarcely be expected to stay away from all the company that had invaded him. Lookers-on, however, had no privileges. In no time at all he found himself hitched in front of the lawn-mower plodding up and down with a resignation that only a donkey can display. Even when we wrapped sacking around his hooves to prevent them marking the turf, he bore it patiently. If they must do these things to him no doubt it was for some purpose, but that purpose lay beyond the comprehension of a humble donkey. He was not to blame for the fact that the sacking slowed his movements so much that we had to remove it.

Somehow, instead of the more usual "I think we shall have to see about that", our tennis court had come into existence within two weeks of its inception and most of the playing season lay ahead. As a family record, that was something indeed.

At the beginning of the century the game had its own character, whether played on the Top Meadow or elsewhere. Recently, revisiting England, I was invited to a delightful tennis party at a farm in the remote countryside in the west of Norfolk. The lawn had been mowed that same afternoon by a motorised mower that whizzed effortlessly over the turf in a matter of minutes, leaving every square foot shorn and smooth. Tea was served in the shade of lusty chestnuts whose sapling days were not of this century or last. The girls — cousins and their friends — turned out, as the expression goes, in white shorts, half sleeve blouses and, of course, no hat — graceful, effective, charming, and most admirably suited for the determined game they were about to play.

But how else would girls turn out for tennis? At that party, as at many another in Australia, my thought flashed to the Top Meadow. There, convention had not as yet recognised any costume as appropriate to the game. Croquet was the genteel game for ladies; it was played in the costume of the garden party — long diaphanous frock that almost swept the turf, blouse with full leg-o-mutton sleeves, wasp waist and wide-brimmed picture hat. So when, about this time, the tennis court began to attract feminine enthusiasts they had no choice but to play in that costume. Sometimes — daring a little — they would take off their hats, but always with a word of excuse for such bold conduct. The young girl in her teens, before she had put up her hair and let down her frocks, was at a much greater advantage. Men and boys of course wore flannels, but not shorts.

And of the game itself. It was unmistakably the game called tennis, for a ball was struck from court to court on opposite sides of a net according to rules which apply to this day. And the score mysteriously started at fifteen and danced in unequal leaps to forty where it was liable to become entangled in a confused maze of "ads" — in or out. If, after some half dozen services, nobody had any strong opinion as to whether or not the score had progressed beyond the forty mark both sides would readily settle for thirty all. This seemed to happen with disconcerting frequency.

The service was sedate. Indeed the over-arm service — and the back-line gymnastics which often accompany it — would have been entirely out of place. The ladies' costume debarred them from attempting it and obviously the gentlemen would not be so unchivalrous as to practice it to their singular advantage. No! — on all Top Meadows the fashion favoured a swinging under-arm service which, although not possessed of the explosive force of the modern service, had developed a fine subtlety of its own. And it was sufficient that the return stroke should be made by thrusting the ball, without malice, in the general direction of the net.

Beyond the western hedge the mill — now stationary after its day's work — spread its wide sails against the slanting rays of the sinking sun. Their shade was most welcome to the players when serving from the far court. From its commanding height on the mill hill, it had surveyed the family comings and goings for close upon two hundred years. It had watched their quiet pastimes down in the garden below — a little mild horticulture on summer evenings with snips and a flower basket; a game of bowls on the lawn for the miller's friends, and later, croquet, demure and restrained for the ladies. Now it gazed down — in astonishment or serenity, who can tell? — on this fresh activity which had come to its meadow in the present generation. This was a more energetic game than any it had seen before; a game where gay young people flitted over the greensward with shrieks of delight when their swipe at the ball was effective, or groans of dismay when it was not. Only the younger girls, unhampered by ankle-length skirts, could play a fast sizzling game.

Surely all this display of energy must call for nourishment. Then let the wind come fair on the morrow and the mill would grind away with merrier zest as its contribution to the pervading gaiety.

The River

Some of the inhabitants of the more elevated parts of the islands of Britain are persuaded that those in Norfolk live in an area which is depressed beneath the level of the sea, that they are entirely surrounded by marsh and fen, by swamp and morass. And, indeed, there is just sufficient of truth in such raillery to make it difficult of reply. Some do live below sea level. There is, in fact, a stretch of marsh to the north-east which is only protected from perpetual inundation from the sea by a ridge of low sand dunes. Since the drainage water will not run uphill from the marshes any more than it will elsewhere, they are drained by a system of dykes from which the water is pumped into the river and so flows away to the sea. The marsh windmill stood ever ready to deal with the surplus water. Its sails were coupled at the base of the mill to a water-wheel running as it were in reverse, and this lifted the water the few feet between the level of the dyke and that of the river. By day as by night, whenever there was a breath of wind, the mill swung to its unending work, seemingly overjoyed if it could race ahead of its fellows dotted over the landscape.

The dunes themselves present a somewhat precarious barrier against the inroads of the sea. The wind, again, is called upon to establish them at the head of the beach beyond the flow of any normal tide. Brushwood hurdles are set up to hold the windswept sand and it is further stabilised by planting the spiky marram grass which thrives under these forbidding conditions and prevents further denudation by the wind.

Ordinarily the waves expend themselves on the long sloping beach before they sweep to the feet of the dunes. But, at high tide, a storm will curl them high up the shore and the dunes may even be breached causing consternation to the dwellers on the marshes.

We must be patient. As recently as the time of the Roman occupation, much more of the county was given over to the wash of the tides. Large estuaries extended far inland. They were later used as sheltered waterways for the raiding vessels of Norseman and Dane. So, perhaps, the passage of yet another two thousand years will see this area raised still further and then no one will need to live below sea level.

The Broadlands of Norfolk remain as a relic of the former tidal estuaries.* Where the sister rivers Yare and Bure flow to the sea at Yarmouth, the tide now sweeps strongly into their lower reaches, although its full effect on the Yare is cushioned by the large expanse of Breydon Water near the mouth of that river. The run of the tide provides an added variety to the pastime of sailing these waters.

* This book was written shortly before it was proved conclusively that the Broads were largely man-made, being the result of medieval peat-digging

If we ignore jibs, spinnakers and the like and confine ourselves solely to the mainsail, the more elementary principles of sailing can be simply stated. A yacht running before the wind — that is, with the wind dead astern — represents the simplest condition. The sail is then run out on either beam until it is truly athwartships and therefore square-on to the wind's direction. The boat is carried along like a leaf before the wind although at a lesser speed because of the resistance offered by the water to the passage of the yacht's hull.

Next, if the wind comes from the beam, the sail in "athwartships" position would obviously catch no wind. It must be hauled until it makes an angle of perhaps thirty degrees with the direction of the yacht's motion. And now, as well as the forward motion through the water we shall make leeway owing to the sideways pressure of the wind.

If the wind moves round still further and blows from dead ahead, we are helpless. No craft can sail dead into the eye of the wind. But, by close-hauling the mainsail, that is by bringing it almost to the fore-and-aft position we can sail very close to the wind. How close depends upon the set of the sail, the fineness of the hull and, be it said, the skill of the yachtsman.

It could scarcely be expected that the wind would be so obliging as to blow from this direction and that expressly to give variety to the yachtsman's sailing. On the Norfolk rivers that entails no disappointment. As he follows their winding course, the yachtsman finds the same wind astern of him, abeam, and ahead all in an hour's cruise. Coming upon the wide expanse of one of the Broads, he may select at will a course that permits him to run before the wind or tack closely into it.

The majestic old schooner of the Broads, the wherry, has succumbed to the inexorable advance of internal combustion. Even the trading wherry, with her brown sail, gliding placidly between meadows of verdant green, was a delight to the eye, but the pleasure wherry reigned supreme as Queen of all the river. On rare occasions her place was challenged by a superlative craft which found its way to these waters from as far abroad as the Mediterranean — an interloper of exquisite form, dressed in a faultless suit of sails, her paintwork without blemish, her professional crew attired in Savile Row yachting uniforms — all of which doubtless gave her grace of standing on the Riviera. But she is overdressed for these homely waters. The wherry loses none of her simple dignity as she moors alongside. Her own brass furnishings and varnished woodwork are everywhere agleam. Her decks are holystoned to a wholesome freshness. Both of the crew — skipper and mate, who is also chief steward — usually wear dark peaked yachting caps and trim blue guernseys, emblazoned across the chest with the wherry's house-flag. They smarten up into whites as the brightness of the day may demand. Their quarters, opening from the aft well, are completely equipped with stove and utensils in the manner of a first-rate commissariat. For'ard of them is the large main saloon fitted with divans along either side and a long central table. For'ard again are isolated double-berth cabins — the whole providing accommodation for a dozen or so holiday-makers. Naturally, deck space is

109

restricted. The general place of assembly is the foredeck ahead of the mast. Here, when sailing, you have an unrestricted view of the river. Here you may take rugs and cushions and read the first page of your book twenty times over betwixt engaging in the chatter around you and watching the life of the river.

Then there are the catwalks leading aft on either side of the saloon hatch. Their true purpose becomes apparent when the wherry, in the absence of wind, has to be travelled under man-propulsion by the aid of the quant poles.

Quanting a 50-ton wherry along cannot be said to be one of the finer arts, but it exercises the body muscles and is not entirely devoid of skill. If a passenger shows an inclination to try his hand at it, the skipper will not discourage him. From a position right for'ard, the long quant is sent almost vertically into the water until it strikes bottom. Then, putting his shoulder to the cap end, the quanter thrusts with all his weight, plodding meanwhile along the cat-walk towards the stern as the wherry moves forward under his feet. He must beware. When he reaches the stern, a good hefty tug will be required to disengage the quant from the mud, sometimes a much stronger tug than is expected. If the quant wins in the tussle, the skipper will not be profoundly amused at having to put into the bank while his quant pole is recovered. He may be highly amused, however, if the quanter goes over the stern still clinging to the quant — more especially if the defaulter happens to be his own mate.

The saloon hatch may be reckoned as deck space only at moorings when all is snugged down. It then makes an excellent place for afternoon tea or those dreamy discussions in the quiet of the evening. When sailing, a cautious skipper watches that none of his passengers uses it unthinkingly, otherwise in a gybe the sweep of the heavy boom across it would be painful to all concerned.

The skipper is wise in the ways of the river. He knows its every reach and bend. This is how his owners came to install him as master of his wherry. But he also fills the position of host to his party, even more so than does the captain of an ocean-going liner. And both he and his owners will feel congratulated if the party asks for himself as skipper on their next holiday.

The young folks love to sit on the hatch by the aft well and encourage the skipper to relate his reminiscences and the profundity of river lore. They question him eagerly and never is he at a loss for a ready reply: "The anchor, Miss? Oh yes, Miss, the mate keeps it under his bunk!" "Snakes, Sir? Not many; land eels we call them around these parts!" Questioning glances in the mate's direction bring neither confirmation nor denial and who can say whether the twinkle in his eye is brighter than usual? Is he not also in training as a wherryman?

When it comes to sailing, the skipper has no difficulty in reverting to his standing as master of the wherry. The party may make its plans, but someone must approach the skipper with them. The breeze that now looks so favourable for a prolonged cruise may not last many days and in that event only much effort with the quant poles will bring him back to the yachting station by the due date. He now makes a brave pretence of his doubts about the weather, but it weakens rapidly under a little cajolery from the young ladies of the party — as he intended from the outset that it should. Sail shall be set!

Of all the sounds that float across the water none is more stirring than the cadence of the windlass as the wherry hoists sail. As a preliminary, the canvas cover under which it is snugged down must be unlashed. The sail itself billows over the hatch as the mate pulls it from its stowage around the boom. Next he shackles the halyards to the gaff and goes for'ard to the windlass. It turns first with easy motion, the pawl rippling over the notches with a clear note softened by reflection from the water. As more and more sail rises from the hatch the pace slackens because of the increasing weight on the halyards. Toward the end, the hoist is taken a notch at a time, under the direction of the skipper who is supervising from his position in the aft well.

The halyards are made fast. The mooring lines are cast. All is clear. The sail fills as the boom is hauled and she glides from her moorings away down the river.

A fine brave picture she makes with black hull, bright woodwork and huge white sail — its high peak reaching above the level of the burgee at the masthead. Lesser craft invariably give her right-of-way, for a crushing impact could only result in disaster to the smaller contestant. None would care to be swept by her heavy boom. In spite of her size she is not ponderous in the water and is possessed of sailing qualities denied to smaller craft. This is said to come about because the peak of her sail reaches to the upper wind where there is less turbulence than at lower levels. Be that as it may, it is a joy to watch her hold a long slant across the river so close to the wind that you constantly expect her to fall away. She makes use of every inch of the river's width before going about. In her case, the rules of sailing do not forbid the use of the quant pole to set her prow over on the opposite tack although, of course, such procedure would be most undignified in handling a yacht.

The river is wide and takes novice and expert alike to its bosom. Without the presence of the "lame duck" it would lose something of its varied attraction. He is at that early stage of development leading to the accomplished yachtsman, where the turn of events is not always as might be intended. He is learning — the hard way. His greatest difficulty seems to come from the fact that his dinghy has no brake lever. What is one to do, careening along under full sail, when an emergency calls for reduced speed, to say nothing of reverse? Perhaps one of the worst hazards — a somewhat unfair one — was the old chain ferry at Horning by which road traffic crossed the river. Approaching it by road from the Woodbastwick side the traveller sounded the bell hung there for the purpose. Thereupon — or more generally in due course — the keeper of the Ferry Inn on the other side of the river showed unmistakable signs of animation and, all in good time, got the punt in motion towards the Woodbastwick side. A chain, normally lying submerged on the river bed, was anchored at either bank. It passed over a sprocket on the deck of the punt so that, when the ferryman wound at his crank, the chain was first drawn taut and then the punt proceeded to cross over as he wound it along the chain.

To those who could read the signal, a red flag at the Ferry Inn gave warning that the punt was at large and enabled them to delay their arrival at the ferry until the river was cleared again. But what of the lame duck, to whom one flag, red though it might be, had no more significance than another. Serenely he bowls around the bend into the Ferry Reach, gaining confidence in the handling of his craft at every turn of the river. The ferryman shouts and gesticulates in his direction. But surely not — it cannot be — that he is being warned not to pass ahead of the punt. Why, at the snail's pace at which it moves, he will have more than half the river's width at his command. The shouting is lost upon him. He continues on. And then suddenly he catches sight of the chain immediately ahead. Heavens! Where is the brake lever? What were those instructions about always turning into the wind upon going about — and where is the wind anyhow? The punt looks so massive; obviously it is not an object to be rammed. In desperation he puts the tiller hard over the wrong way. The boom gybes with a violence calculated to decapitate any who stand within its sweep; he sprawls into the well barely in time to escape its murderous intent, leaving the yacht headed across the river. It finishes with its prow reared up on the quay of the Ferry Inn, its shrouds entangled in the branches of an overhanging willow tree.

The first lesson was unreasonably complicated. Yet it is amazing how persistent is that tendency to misuse the tiller. In a restricted fairway it is disconcerting, if no

114

more, to find a craft bearing down upon you and, just as you expect her to sheer off a little, her tiller is eased to the left in the fond belief that she will steer in that direction. So are born those subtle pleasantries in circumstances which cannot be adequately met by an air of detached indifference.

Yet everyone must pass through the lame duck stage before he may call himself a yachtsman, and surely it is the most exhilarating period of all. How in later life shall the joy of those early days be recaptured? A bellying sail, a fluttering pennant, must always spell delight but in the glad days of youth they spell more — they hold enchantment. To stand upon your own quarter-deck, tiny though it be, to sense the tug of the sheet in a goodly breeze and the strong thrust of the tiller. To see the mast careen to every fitful gust and watch the water swirl to the heeling deck, to feel the doubt that you may be holding her too close to the wind, to think that disaster may suddenly crack down upon you. These quicken the pulse. They sharpen the wits.

At her launching the ocean-going liner slides majestically down the ways to her element to the accompaniment of grand ceremony. It would be pleasing to think that the entitlement to these rites is not governed by size alone — that even a small yacht, lithesome and dainty, should dip to the water for the first time to some light formality at which she is given the name she is to bear so long as she shall remain upborne upon the water — "I name thee *Whitewing* and may joy come to those who sail under the spread of thy canvas".

At any rate, the yacht that you charter months ahead of the cruise is known to you at that time only by name. Truly enough the catalogue describes her as "28-footer, well found, with accommodation for four" and upon that bare statement arrangements are made and hopes ride high.

Slowly the weeks go by and then it is only days before you report at the yachting station to claim your charter. So far, none of those secret anxieties which have assailed you have taken shape — that some mishap on a previous cruise, some chance of the weather even, might result in the unavoidable cancellation of the yacht's charter. But not until you have actually stepped aboard can they be entirely dismissed. So some trepidation is mingled with repressed excitement as the party assembles, each burdened with the equipment which has been assigned to him as his contribution to the general well-being.

And then you glimpse her — *Whitewing* — lying moored amongst a fleet of her sister craft. Ah! misgivings are over. All has befallen as planned. Henceforth for a space you belong to the river.

On that first evening afloat, it is sufficient to draw away from the bustle and congestion of the yachting station to a quiet mooring some few miles down the river. There, the yacht's economy may be explored before nightfall. The accommodation on a 28-footer is restricted but, even so, that is part of the fun. After they have become accustomed to moving about with stooping shoulders, the ladies will enjoy the luxury of the comparatively spacious cabin and its cushioned bunks.

The men will fend as best they may — one on a shakedown in the well, and the other in a cubby hole in the forepeak ahead of the mast.

Just now there is excitement over the preparation of the evening meal. It proceeds to the accompaniment of exclamations at the cunning stowages for crockery and utensils. Much advice is forthcoming on the caprices of a primus stove and the way to humour it. Most of it is wasted however, since the one in question is not to be deterred from boiling water in the way it has always done. And, inevitably, it is discovered that some article which "we must take" has been forgotten. The culprit flounders in search of an alibi but, protest as he may, cannot absolve himself. His offer to return for it and rejoin the party on the following day is met with gay derision. Hunger will not wait upon such an impossible diversion.

Twilight deepens and the yacht must be snugged down. The boom, resting in its crutch on the counter, is contrived to form the ridge pole for an awning which converts the well into an enclosed adjunct to the cabin. When all is secured and the oil lamp is lighted, a cosiness is engendered which neither wind nor rain can penetrate. The moorings, too, have been happily chosen. Two or three other craft lie alongside the staithe at a little distance. But they are peaceful folk. Only an occasional ripple of laughter from them comes over the water to be dissolved into the stillness of the evening.

And now, as night settles down, it is well to take a last look around before turning in. From the staithe the little craft is seen lying snug upon the dark surface of the water. Only a glow worm's glint, coming from the cabin lamp, filters through the canvas awning. All beyond is enveloped in the faintest starshine of a still summer's night. The mast of a yacht moored on the far side of the river can be just discerned standing sentinel over those who slumber at its foot. A little way upstream the village lies at rest. Its few remaining lights shine dimly from candles set at this hour in upstairs windows and they too will soon be extinguished.

But hark now, from down the silent river comes the sound of intermittent splashing. It is too loud for a moorhen's sputter and if it comes from some nocturnal swimmer he must surely be in difficulty. What should be done? He may be in danger of drowning. Even while you hesitate, the sound grows louder and presently all doubts are resolved as a belated yachtsman out in midstream gropes his way through the darkness with a quant pole. He must have badly misjudged his distance from a mooring or else has suffered a mishap which prevented him from getting in before sundown. Now close upon midnight, like a Charon, he ferries his Stygian craft over the black water to an unknown destination. His shadowy outline is faintly visible for but a few moments until it is swallowed up again by the night. His sinister splashing fades away with him. After he has passed, the silence is broken only by the crake of a distant nightjar or the longdrawn hoot of an owl. These and the soft friendly slap-slap of tiny wavelets under the yacht's bow at your feet which must now lull everyone to sleep.

The blush of dawn steals up over a countryside drenched in dew and scented with meadowsweet. A thin mist rises from the low marshes stretching away from the river bank and there the cattle are already quietly cropping the lush pasture. Except for them, no living thing is stirring. Over the river itself the mist gathers somewhat more densely and there the yachts lie in repose, strung out along the bank. Their masts reach mutely skyward and the pennants droop limply as though they likewise have not yet received the call to awaken. Dew lies heavy upon the awnings. Sleep still claims those who shelter beneath.

Yet a little while and the light strengthens. The gentle hues dissolve before the sun's dilated orb as it sweeps up to ride full and majestic over the horizon. And now some slight activity breaks upon the river. First a small boy from the village who has been restlessly awaiting the first glimmer of daylight to fit a new sail to his dinghy comes barefoot along the road past the line of yachts with the canvas bundled across his shoulders. And soon an old salted wherryman emerges from his cuddy and lustily scents the morning air. He casts around the sky to see what the day may hold in store and then with deliberation takes bucket and mop to expunge the mud streaks from the hull of his wherry where he brushed the bank the previous evening. He prefers that when the river awakens they shall not be in evidence to call forth any caustic comment on his sailing.

These early risers, however, are few. The sun is half way to the zenith before the majority of the floating population is astir. By that time the morning is sparkling fresh, with a soft wind blowing. The surface of the water is dancing and the tufted rushes sway to it from the bank in graceful accompaniment.

On the river, lunch is a picnic affair at which sandwiches are passed around whilst the yacht is on the move or perhaps laid up by the bank wherever the party happens to find itself at the time when someone insists that food comes next. Dinner, too, is a feast which is movable anywhere within a range of three or four hours depending on those incidents of the day that cannot be catered for. But breakfast time finds nearly all craft clustered at moorings within reach of the amenities of a village. And breakfast, at an improvised table set up in the well, is a delectable meal under the open sky with the river in full view. Each member of the party will have had some responsibility in its preparation, from the lowly one of fetching paraffin for the primus stove to the momentous decision that the kippers are cooked. If there should be a culinary disaster, everyone is sure to be implicated. But high spirits and gay surroundings lighten any and all such contretemps.

At this hour there is a deal of movement on road and river. Bevies of smiling youngsters troop along to the village, bent upon the inconsequential shopping. Menfolk fetch water and the more bulky stores. The village dairyman comes to the yachts with the morning's milk. The cottager's small boy comes alongside in an enormously disproportionate punt with punnets of fruit picked fresh from the garden.

This, too, is the youngsters' hour on the river when they may exercise their yachtsmanship in the dinghy whilst their elders are busied with affairs of breakfast on the yacht — not that they will venture out of range of the signal which will call them to the meal. Two small boys yet to enter their teens give a laudable display of clean sailing as they tack up the river. The breeze is just smart enough to liven the dinghy's movements and keep them on the alert. Presently they become aware of another dinghy a hundred yards below them. It is manned by a slip of a girl, no older than themselves, clad in bright cerise sweater and stocking cap. And, although neither would deign to acknowledge the presence of the other, it is well seen that a juvenile regatta is staged. The boys become a little more careful to get the best slant across the river. Honour must be upheld, especially as there are two of them and only one girl. But missy is overhauling them. Her hand bears lightly on the tiller as she goes about. Her handling of the sail is perfection. She skirts the bank on each tack with the slightest margin but is calm and confident withal, a little yachtswoman deserving of the costume she wears.

On such a day the yachts will sail unreefed, of that there is no question. One by one they draw away. You may almost dream yourself along between the meadows on either side. There is just a pleasant sound of the surge of water under the bow which only emphasises the pervading peace and quiet. The yacht will almost sail herself, she is docile and contented. She asks only that in tacking you do not subject her to the indignity of drawing on to the bank; that in running you at least cast an occasional glance under the boom to see that you are not heading into someone in a more somnolent state than yourself. Even the swing of the boom in a gybe is without malice. And at any time you may heave to at the bank by freeing the sail and heading her into the breeze.

There are, of course, those other days when the wind blows boisterous and gusty at nearly gale force, when it might have been wiser to reef the mainsail but you decide with some hesitation that she can just be managed under full canvas. Now she must be watched and handled aright — and no nonsense. On a close-hauled tack the thrust of the tiller will demand the whole effort of the helmsman and the tug and snatch of the sheet will fully extend another crew member. An unpremeditated gybe will be the only one allowed to you — at any rate on that trip. But this is sailing and there is zest in it. There is satisfaction in making headway against the wind up one of the narrower waterways. With only two or three boat lengths on the shorter leg of a tack, it is easy enough to lose way and get blown hard into the rushes to leeward — an unenviable predicament for the only way out of it is to lower sail, quant against the wind to the other side and start afresh. Since you then have no way on at all, there is every possibility of repeating the performance several times over. The wind is persistently unhelpful. Such are among the less exhilarating episodes of sailing.

And again there are those days when no yachts sail. When, upon waking, the steady patter of rain on the awning impels you to lie snug in your bunk for another hour. Eventually murmurs from the interior of the cabin indicate that breakfast cannot be indefinitely deferred. Someone must bestir themselves. In a spirit of sublime chivalry you decide it may as well be yourself. The prospect when you part the flaps of the awning is not inviting. Rain splashes ceaselessly upon the water. Each drop bounces a tiny pinnacle from its own miniature crater and the pattern quivers in endless repetition as far as the gaze can penetrate. The yachts lie, forlorn and comatose, at their moorings. Occasionally a cloaked figure emerges and trudges stolidly down the road. Otherwise it is entirely deserted.

But, having cast your lot upon the river, you must not be impatient of its moods. On such a day the cabin, which up to then had appeared to be reasonably spacious, contracts rapidly in every dimension until, drizzle or deluge, you must have breathing space. One by one, the members of the party are inveigled into agreement with the proposal for a long walk. And, surprisingly, the long tramp through drenched country lanes proves to be a most satisfying excursion. Saturation point for clothes and footwear is quickly reached and, after that, much rain or little is of no consequence. There is joy in defying the weather, in challenging the rain to dampen the exuberance of the party.

To Horsey Mere the zealous yachtsman turns as the Moslem turns to Mecca. Perhaps it intrigues him to sail up the river to the sea instead of down, for the farther shore lies yet a crow's mile from the salt waters of the North Sea, although it does not connect with it. Perhaps the pilgrimage is irresistible because of the engaging names of the waterways that take him there. For who so cold as not to glow at the prospect of sailing from the River Bure to the River Thurne and on to Potter Heigham, of slanting across landlocked Heigham "Sound" (as though, for the nonce, he were a deep-sea mariner), of booming along between the green banks of the narrow Meadow Dyke to emerge suddenly on to the broad expanse of Horsey Mere itself.

Its rush-fringed shores give no encouragement as a mooring, and so the yachts tie up in the Meadow Dyke by the road just at the entrance to the Mere. But, so narrow is the Dyke, that they take up nearly half its width, leaving little enough water for a yacht under sail to pass. That, however, is not manifest to the uninitiated until he is almost upon them. And so, on a certain day, the situation thereabouts was fraught with anxious tension. The wind was strong — so strong as to induce some four or five yachts to lie up in the Meadow Dyke rather than take what risk there might be in spreading their canvas to it. Down the Dyke another yacht — not so cautious — came spanking along heeled well over, with the boom full out on the beam. Although he had sighted the line of masts from a distance there was no suggestion then of impending danger. Coming round the bend of the Dyke he saw too late that serious trouble was inescapable. The boom was out on that side where the moored yachts lay. It would rake the whole line of them just above the cabin tops. Hauling it in would only have the effect of causing his own mast to careen over to a greater angle and already it must strike the stationary masts. The dilemma was complete. Only seconds remained however in which any evasive action could be taken. Those on board the moored yachts took their own. They either leapt ashore or dived down into the well to escape the onslaught of the murderous boom. In desperation rather than by design, those on board the

124

charging yacht took what proved to be the best possible course. Gauging matters to a nicety they paid out the boom instead of hauling in. This reduced the heel-over of their own mast so that it just cleared that of the first stationary yacht. Immediately afterwards they hauled the boom so that its impact was reduced. The blow caused the stationary yacht to lurch badly, but rigging and gear suffered no actual breakage. So! the first hazard was overcome. But the other yachts lay ahead — this was no time to contemplate what might have been. Each of them in turn was treated in the same way — pay out the boom to ensure the masts did not clash, haul in quickly to reduce the impact of the boom.

The last yacht took the worst punishment. Moreover its crew had the opportunity of watching the whole course of events and were, therefore, in readiness to express their feelings as the charging yacht shot clear into the open waters of the Mere. Did they call after him "Well done, old man! You got out of that with superb yachtsmanship?" Let truth and honesty prevail. They did not. They were rude, not to say coarse, about the yacht's boom, beam and bluster. They offered suggestions as to where it might well repose at that present time. Their remarks grew fainter as the intervening distance increased but were understood to make reference to oars, rowlocks and crabs. So may the merit of the most brilliant achievement be lost upon those whose part is that of the injured spectator.

The lure of Horsey Mere, however, cannot be permitted to cloud the judgement. It is many a long mile from the yachting station at Wroxham and the rule there is rigid that Saturday noon is surrender hour for the yacht. That dire penalty may await those who ignore is best left unexplored — too dreadful the thought of being black-listed against any future cruise. Well enough if, when returning from Horsey, the other side of the breeze that brought you will be so considerate as to take you back again. But what if the doldrums descend? Movement in a homeward direction can then come only from the thrust of the quant pole or the tug of the tow rope — and much hard walking must accompany either. After an hour spent on the end of a tow rope the water that purled under the bow in a fresh breeze becomes as the most viscous treacle. And, moreover, your charming companion at the tiller has evidently conspired against you. She holds the yacht so far out from the bank that the tow is taken at an uncomfortably obtuse angle except when, upon a tactful correction from yourself, she steers so close in that the hull drags against the bank and increases the resistance fourfold. It becomes impossible to refrain from the suggestion that it helps a lot to watch what you are doing. And it is at this precise moment, of course, as though to give emphasis to your remarks, that you stumble into a ditch and besmear yourself with mud from ankle to elbow. Now the situation becomes really complicated. It is obvious you were so intent on watching what someone else was doing that you failed to apply the advice to yourself and to keep your mind on "just pulling the boat along". Life from the shore end of a tow rope is fraught with many discouragements.

By one means or another, sail, tow or quant, the yacht reaches her last mooring on the Friday evening within mallard flight of Wroxham. These last hours afloat are too precious to spend straightening up in readiness for the handover. That may be left to the morning and an early rising.

How shall you become inured again to an existence without booms and halyards? How forego the long days spent under the open sky? How to be contented where no water is? But on the morrow you must. These things have, in so short a time, become the very essence of existence, yet they must be forsaken.

But we may go a-wandering in the twilight of this last evening on an expedition that will rejoice the heart. Close at hand, lying amidst the woods, is the gem village of the Broadlands. From the river the pathway winds away between water-filled dykes whose banks are fringed with lush marshland verdure. Their green is flecked with the yellow of wild iris and marshmallow. They are perfumed with the heady scent of meadowsweet. Presently a turnstile straddles the path and gives on to a country lane whose leafy charm heralds the loveliness of the village itself. For when you come upon it, it is set as in a picture frame.

Farmhouses and cottages and church are there built back a little from the greenest of village greens. And in this place, so close to where the thatching rushes grow, how else should they be snuggled down but with thatch, the gables springing sharp-ridged from the splay of the roof. They frame the lattice windows retiring shy beneath sloping eaves. Only in these gardens do hollyhocks reach so high with delphiniums striving their utmost to surpass them. Without, upon the green and around the church, English chestnuts lord their shapely magnificence over the tapering yews.

Now is peace and sleep comes quickly. Tomorrow we shall make ready the yacht for those who are to follow us. Treat her fair and she will dance to the frolic of the breeze. She will bring halcyon days to those who love her and, ourselves, we shall surely claim her grace again.

Twice each day the appearance of Breydon Water alternates between an inland lake some five miles by one in extent, and an expanse of uninviting mudflats through which the river Yare has its course to the sea. Much water flows and ebbs at each tide. The moon has but six hours to flow the water from the Harbour Mouth at Yarmouth and over the mudflats at Breydon to a depth of some three or four feet. And the same water must ebb to the sea again in the succeeding six hours. In consequence, when the tide is in full rip below Breydon, it runs at a rate of some six or seven knots. The same conditions determine that slack water between tides is of short duration. Breydon Water, therefore, has no enticement for the yachtsman. It holds for him the wretched possibility of getting stuck fast on the mud and remaining there, anxious and uncomfortable, for six hours until the next tide shall refloat him. It holds also the real danger of getting caught in the rip at Yarmouth and being swirled swiftly and helplessly under the road bridge. Of the evils which can then befall, the lesser is for the mast to be snapped off by the arches overhead. The greater is for the mast to hold and in doing so cause the yacht to be swamped and capsized as the rip carries it forward beneath the arches. Though the struggling yachtsman may then be fortunate enough to escape entanglement in the sail, the swirl of water is ruthless in its efforts to engulf him.

However, the north river, the Bure, can only be reached from any point on the Yare by crossing Breydon and so coming to the confluence of the two rivers at Yarmouth.

Here it was that three of us brothers came very near to tragedy. The eldest of us was a bare sixteen and none could be said to have graduated from the lame-duck stage. A friend had made us the offer of a yacht, lying at Brundall on the Yare. It was that or nothing for a holiday on the river that year. But, to us, the Yare was less interesting than the Bure at Wroxham and Horning and we badly wanted to do our sailing there. Could we sail her the 20 miles or so down the Yare, across Breydon and up the Bure to Horning? Parental agreement had, of course, to be obtained and at first this appeared to offer an insurmountable difficulty. "But we would be so careful", there were three of us to handle the boat when really only two were required. This was our only chance for a cruise on the river this summer. "Please, we know we shall be all right."

We knew, vaguely enough I fear at that age, of the tides at Yarmouth. So, upon leaving Brundall we worked out the time we might expect to arrive at Yarmouth and checked from the newspaper that it would then be slack water. We should make the mouth of the Bure on the slack and have the flow of the tide to carry us well up its lower reaches before nightfall.

The scheme was perfect if only we had kept to our plan. It was upset by the too-favourable wind which brought us to the head of Breydon Water some two or three hours earlier than our calculations had forecast. We laid up and deliberated. The mud banks of Breydon were still covered with water but, seeing that the channel was so well defined by marker posts, surely we could keep to it. The tide had evidently just turned and the sting would have gone from it by the time we had crossed Breydon. If we waited for the slack we should be in this insalubrious spot for another three hours. The deliberations were not over-prolonged; we hauled the sheet to the wind and drew away.

Sure enough, by making the tacks a good deal shorter than was actually necessary, we had no difficulty in keeping to the channel. Our ultra care, however, did once lead to minor trouble of another sort. This happened as we passed a trading wherry, the only other sail on Breydon that day. He, knowing the water blindfold, was tacking the full width between markers and was not prepared, as we passed him, for our shorter tacks. We cleared him by a boat's length but he hailed us with the promise of the "thick end" if we got abreast of him again. The remark was unnecessarily discouraging, had he but known the tense condition of our nerves.

Otherwise all was going well and presently we had passed under the railway swing bridge and were on the lookout for the entrance to the Bure. Yes, this must be it, with a specially prominent marker post apparently somewhat out of line. According to the practice which had up to now served us so well we would give it a wide berth.

What with the running tide and a good breeze, we were scudding along fast. And then came disaster — fierce and sudden. We had gone the wrong side of the marker. We had taken the mud bank full tilt. In an instant the yacht heeled to her beam ends. All of us, like everything else in the boat, were thrown forward and one brother slid into the water but managed to hold on. There we lay at a most unhealthy angle, with the sail flat on the water. Had we not struck so hard the gurgling tide might have swept us off the mud to fresh disaster, but our initial error had the virtue that it was very direct and very strong.

With returning wits, it was obvious that the sail must first be got inboard. Wet as it was, this was not achieved without a big struggle. The boom still dangled in the water but the situation seemed to be under some sort of control. Next, we tried to push the yacht back into the channel by thrusting with the quant pole at the bow. That proved to be hopeless for we had nothing but the mud to thrust against and then only with the spike end of the quant. In any event, it was entirely the wrong thing to do. For, had we forced her from the mud, we should have been at the mercy of the current and must inevitably have been swept under the low road bridge and have been capsized. We were at least afloat but, to three boys, the situation could scarcely have been more depressing. What of those assurances we had given at home that we could look after ourselves? How soon we had failed — and one of us so nearly lost overboard.

And then from the shore, some two hundred yards away, we were hailed by a boatman who signalled us that he would come. How could he possibly reach us in a rowboat across that swirl of water? But he knew the vagaries of the current and where it ran less viciously. We saw him take his boat well upstream. Then, rowing hard against the current, he yet drifted down to us by a devious course. Never it seemed was help more welcome.

Presently he reached us. Had we a 56 lb weight to cast overboard on a line? An anchor was useless in the mud. No? "Well, you should never come to this water without one, miboys. But never mind, we'll get you to the bank all right, though it would have been easier with the weight."

He showed us how to thrust sideways with the quant and disturb the mud under the bow so that the current helped in scouring it away. After a while, she came to a more even keel and he made to take us in tow. But again, when we eventually came free, he did not attempt to reach the shore directly. He smelt out the slack water over the shoals and edged this way and the other until we lay under the lee of the bank. The danger had passed. We made to recompense him but he would not hear of it.

It was a subdued and chastened trio that surveyed the situation. We must yet face the perils of Breydon again because, after the cruise, the yacht must be tied up at the starting point, Brundall. But at least we knew that we could never make the same mistake again. When, at the end of a week, we did make the return trip we were possessed of the confidence which seven days cruising had given us and could jest at our earlier misfortune. We even found it in our hearts to wish that Breydon were not quite so placid. Upon reaching home the experience had so faded into the past as to be scarcely worth mentioning. Had we not said we could look after ourselves!

Sunday

Sunday was a pleasant day at the Mill House. There was a Medic law that everyone — elders and youngsters alike — must go to the parish church in the morning, but the pleasure and excitement of the day started much earlier. From the moment of awakening, the Sunday feeling was with you — a stillness out of doors which itself encouraged the thrush perched on the topmost branches of the sweet-apple tree to trill, over and over, every note in his repertoire. There were soft thuddings from remote parts of the house which told that others were a-stir and searching for clean fresh clothing which somehow always seemed to get mixed up with your brothers'. These things were themselves exhilarating.

Downstairs, there was a bustling in the kitchen that only Sunday brought and, so that you might not be late, you hurried outside to do your "turns" — to feed the rabbits or bantams or to lead the donkey up to the Top Meadow.

Who would care to be late for breakfast on Sunday morning, even if he dared? Who would dare to be late, even if he wished? Although nobody thought of it in that way, this was a family parade, and any excuses were worse than none at all.

A good deal of scuffling went on as everyone got seated at the large table — parents at either end, of course, and six youngsters looking across it from either side — most likely to be eight of them if it happened to be holiday time, because then a couple of cousins would almost certainly be staying at the Mill House.

A few corrections, friendly but not to be ignored, would come from behind the tea-tray and the immense array of cups and saucers surrounding it. How else would a semblance of order be maintained in a high-spirited family? And my Father would come in for his share of them too. He was, I think, never so happy as when presiding at his end of the table and joining in whimsical fashion in the chatter and fun that passed around.

Oatmeal porridge from a huge tureen was served first. Much of our provisioning for the table came from the mill or the large garden; cereal, eggs and all manner of vegetables and fruit. The economy of the groceries required that damaged grain, sweepings and siftings should not be allowed to go to waste and this, of itself, demanded that the pig sties were always inhabited. Twice a year, therefore, a litter of piglets came from one of our farmers. When they were grown and fatted ready for market one was always "killed into the house". My Mother did the salting down. Afterwards, the flitches went to the city for curing. So there was always a supply of bacon hanging in mutton-cloth bags in the larder.

If the chatter was somewhat hushed when the large plates of porridge were passed around, it was not for long. There were at least as many different topics to be

135

discussed as there were seats at the table. Certainly there were times when confusion became imminent and then complete silence would be called from the head of the table, upon pain that an offender should stand down and leave the room. And now a quandary rested with each and every one. We knew what silence meant, and also that there was no room for equivocation in complying with the terms as issued. Yet how could Sunday morning breakfast be despoiled of all there was to tell and hear. It was beyond human endurance — at any rate that of small humans. So silence reigned for just so long as it took someone to raise his courage and try out the atmosphere: "Could I have a little salt, please?" If he got away with it, if he had not overlooked the salt already on his plate, harmony would be restored by tentative approaches to more engaging subjects. More frequently than not it worked.

After the oatmeal came sausages and bacon, without which Sunday morning would have been dull indeed. The miller had a standing order to call for sausages at a village shop some five miles away where the butcher fattened his own pigs. As he never had any other meat in the shop, the content of his sausages was beyond question. He was deservedly famous. Though his name be forgotten the remembrance of his sausages must be graven on the memory of each of the youngsters.

Soon after breakfast preparations were made to start for church. Amongst the youngsters it was largely a question of who was going to walk with whom and when each would be ready to leave.

How came Sprowston Church to be built where it is? It was almost two miles from the village proper, nearly as far as it could possibly be while still remaining within the parish boundary. Could it be that it was intended to lie centrally amidst the farms of Old Sprowston. If so, they nearly all had the same distance to walk as the village people. Yet, there it was, right out in the country, off the main highway, two miles from everybody. This is however but a passing reflection. No one would have wished it otherwise.

Indeed, the two-mile walk to and from church was part of the day's delight. If it was raining hard, you had an inner feeling of nobility as you trudged along, a feeling of martyrdom in a good cause. You were sustained by the thought that, of a certainty, the folks from Old Sprowston would be there and how, therefore, could you let the Village down by asking permission to stay at home on account of a splash of rain?

On a fine summer's day you set out gladly enough, just one mile along the highway, quiet and still on this bright morning, past open fields and woods and then the turn at the kissing-gate on to the footpath leading through standing corn, to the church in the distance.

The family pews in church were allocated according to a most proper order of precedence. On our side of the centre aisle, the front pew went to the "Hall" and the one behind to the "Lodge". The Mill House came about halfway down, but there were too many of us to fit into one pew. We mostly overflowed to the side aisle. Across the centre aisle was first the "Vicarage", then the "Manor" and, almost level with us but slightly in front "White Hall Farm". Its large family occupied two pews, elders behind and younger members in front where they were under observation. I think we were in the more favourable strategic position because we could look across and watch any unorthodox incidents which occurred there, but they could only see us by turning half round at the risk of drawing upon themselves a corrective prod from behind. The conditions were highly satisfactory to the Mill House.

However, these were but minor distractions from the grandeur of the service. The vicar, at all times a kindly and genial man, was no less so when performing his high office. His fine features and upright bearing gave added dignity to his exalted duty. Through his rich melodious voice, the word of the prophets rang out with clear decision. His sermons spoke of things noble and homely. Sprowston was a small village, its church was isolated, but in its vicar it was blessed with a man of rare understanding.

At that time it did not call for remark, at least not a remark of disapprobation, if her ladyship from the Hall was driven to church in her phaeton or, in winter, the closed carriage — nor if others from a distance drove up in a pony chaise. On rare occasions, some of us from the Mill House would do so. Each, in its ways, was a modest conveyance and not inappropriate for use on Sunday morning. But there was a delicacy in such matters. No one, for instance, would contemplate driving to church in a dog-cart. It was altogether too jaunty for the occasion. Only those people from the far extremity of Sprowston, who mostly lived in London and consequently could not appreciate the affront they gave to local sensitivity, would use the dog-cart on Sunday.

Much later, forty years later, I sat for a brief hour in the old Mill House pew, my daughter beside me, herself a grown young person in her early twenties. When I closed my eyes in meditation, it would surely be vouchsafed to me that I might allow my mind to wander back over the years that had gone and reflect upon the present amazing circumstances.

My work in England was finished, my stay was over. Throughout the summer, both Shirley and I had had our own affairs to attend to but we had managed to spend several weekends in company upon various pilgrimages. And now, although she was staying on, this was my last Sunday in England and it was doubtful if I should ever return. In four days' time I should have passed through Cairo, Karachi and Calcutta and be at work again in a busy modern city on the opposite side of the world. But, today, we sat in Sprowston Church — myself who had sat there as a boy so often before, my daughter for the first time.

The family was scattered, but, of them all, only one, my father, had been laid to rest and he now lay with his forebears in the churchyard outside. This was my own village, my birthplace. My name was written in the volume of the book kept in this very place. These were my people who spoke that broad dialect which, travel wide as you may, you will not hear in any other corner of the world. At that hour, the years that had passed between were as a dream in the night.

We had come early and I had spoken to the churchwarden as we went in. He was of my generation and insisted that Shirley and I must sit in the old family seat. As the congregation gathered to the church I saw only one amongst them whom I had known in the years that were gone. He sat in the White Hall Farm pew.

It was evident from the glances of those around us that they wondered who were the strangers, an elderly man and a young girl, seated amongst them that morning, gladly welcome as they were. But, although we may have had the appearance of strangers, I knew myself to be the native and those others the strangers. I saw the church through half closed eyes peopled with another generation. The bells rang out the same changes over the fields. The morning sun, streaming through the windows, cast the same coloured patterns that it had always done. The boys' voices from the choir rang as ever to the rafters. And there in miniature, in a recess by the north wall, knelt Christopher Knolles in prayers as he had done since the first Elizabeth ruled the land. Behind him knelt his six sons in proper precedence of birthright and opposite, the Lady Knolles and three daughters. Wars had come and the distractions of a modern age but here, in this country church set amongst the fields, forty years were but as yesterday.

I must perforce take leave of the village — my village — and go my ways as Providence has decreed. Yet the memory of those other days is secure. I know that, whatever changes may be noticeable to the eye, the pattern of life there will remain unaltered down the years that are to come.

Herbert Clifford Harrison,
Esperance Avenue,
Brighton, Victoria, Australia.

The Author

The author was born at the Mill House, Sprowston in 1888. Inspired by the engineering skill of craftsmen of an earlier age, typified in the works of the mill, he himself chose engineering as a profession, but in the sphere of aircraft production. He became an associate of the Royal College of Science, Kensington, in 1908, and after an appointment in England went to Melbourne as an assistant engineer to a harvester company. He held appointments in the technical services with the RAAF and the RAF, and with the Commonwealth Aircraft Corporation, Melbourne. He was recalled to the RAAF for war service in 1942 and was appointed Superintendent of Airworthiness and Aeronautical Engineering, Department of Civil Aviation, Melbourne in 1946.

Sprowston Mill and its Owners

Sprowston Mill was built in 1730 and accidentally destroyed by fire on March 24th 1933. It was then one of the last post mills surviving in England.

In 1842 Robert Robertson, aged 48, was killed when he became entangled in the drive from the head wheel to his own sack hoist. His wife, Sarah, became the owner of the mill and their second son, George, became the miller and remained so until his death in 1884. He was unmarried and left no children. George Robertson's elder sister, Elizabeth, had married William Harrison in 1849 and they had one daughter, Clara, and seven sons, the "Seven Wonders". The second of the sons, William Albert, took over Sprowston mill in 1884 on the death of his Uncle George. This William Harrison married his childhood sweetheart, Rachel Linford, and they had two daughters and four sons. The second of these sons, Herbert Clifford, is the author of this book and also of "The Story of Sprowston Mill" published in 1949. Both books were written to help his father recover from his distress at the burning of the mill. William Albert Harrison continued to work Sprowston mill until he retired in 1920 and then hired the mill to his third son, Horace, who was the last working miller of Sprowston.

A few years after the fire of 1933, a small housing estate was built over the site of the mill. Mill House remains, in a state of dilapidation, but the site of the mill itself is covered by a substantial modern bungalow, 41 Windmill Court. The present occupant and her husband took up residence in 1977. She says that from time to time she was aware of a "presence" in the hall of the bungalow. In her mind she christened him "Robert".

Sometimes she actually saw a shortish, stout man, in "ordinary working clothes" and once he spoke her name. She has always felt his presence was friendly and seemed to guarantee her safety in the house, especially so after the death of her husband. Later she read "The Story of Sprowston Mill" and has often wondered whether she is seeing the ghost of Robert Robertson who was killed in the mill in 1842.

The Mechanisms of the Mill

Drawings by Graham Nisbet

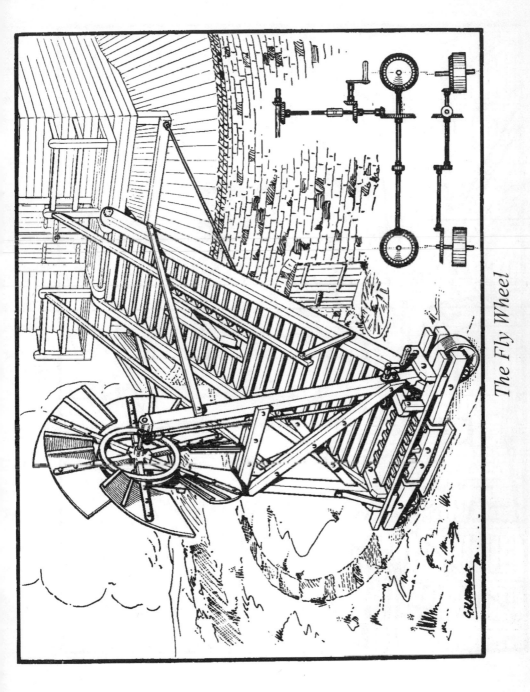

The Fly Wheel

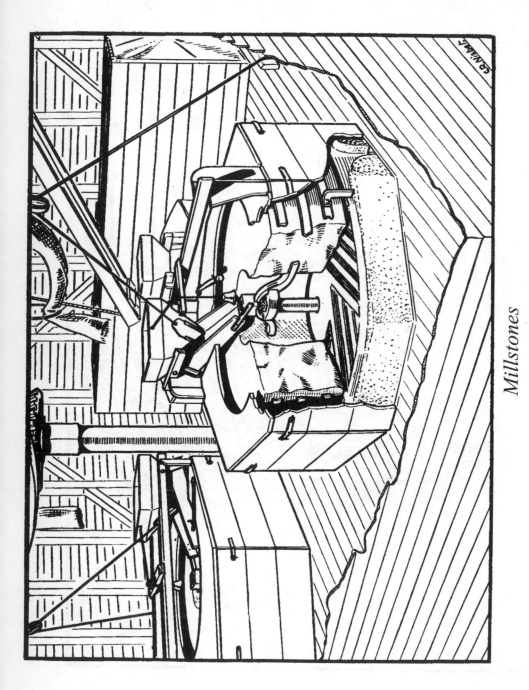

Millstones

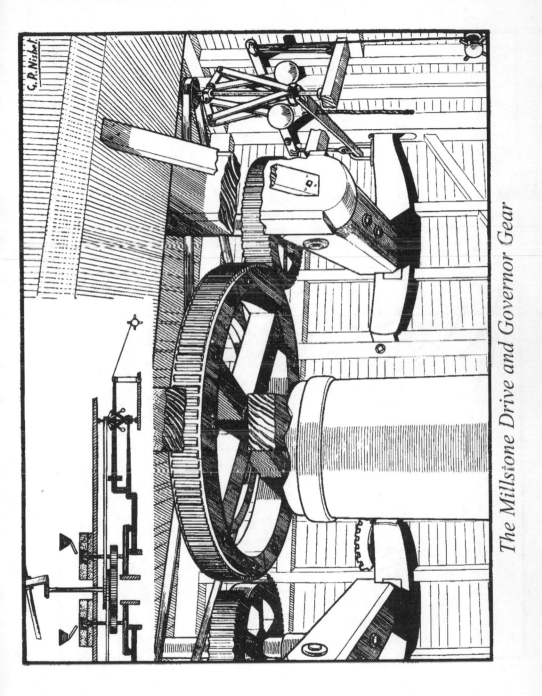

The Millstone Drive and Governor Gear

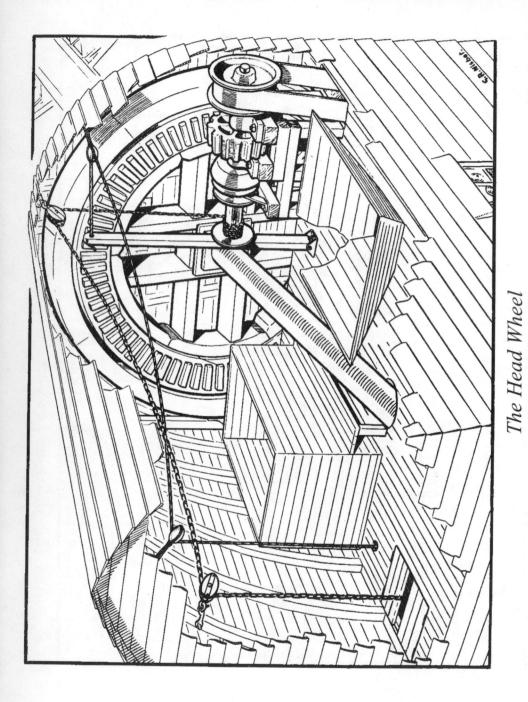

The Head Wheel

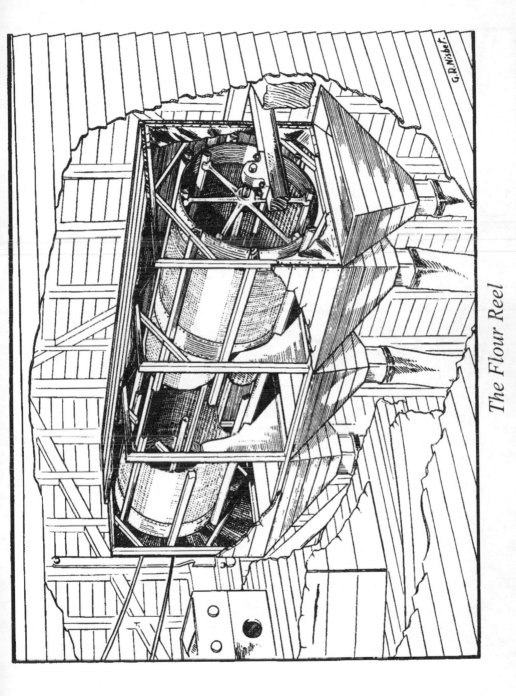

The Flour Reel

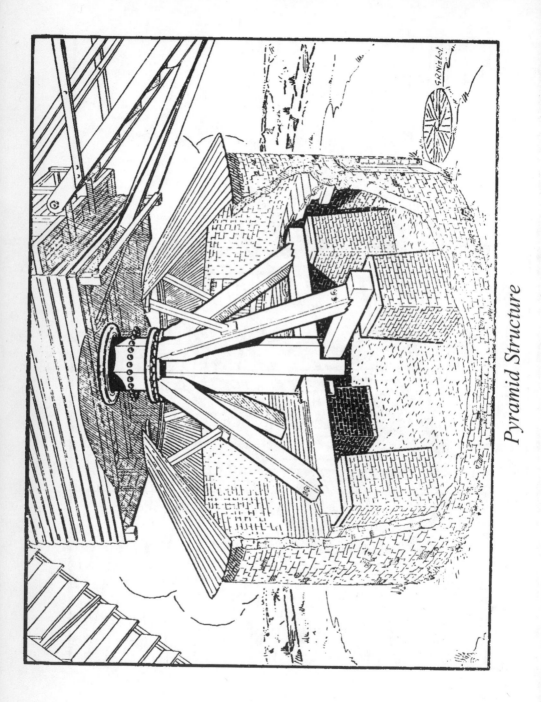

Pyramid Structure

Layout — Millstones and Reel Floor

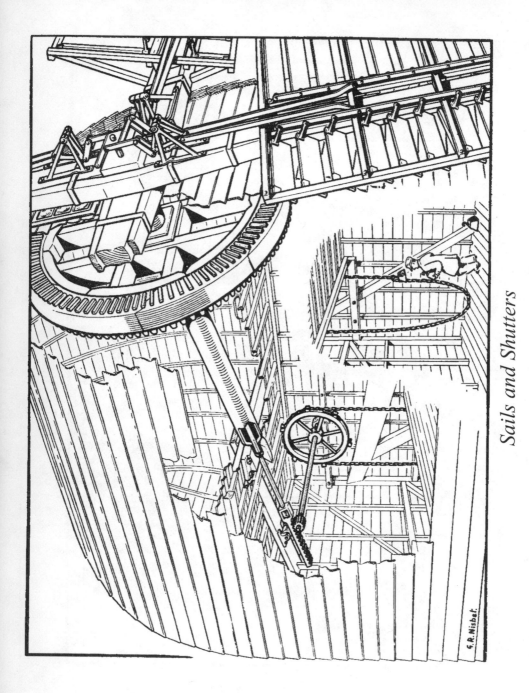

Sails and Shutters

E.R.Nisbet.

ISIS publish a wide range of books in large print, from fiction to biography. A full list of titles is available free of charge from the address below. Alternatively, contact your local library for details of their collection of ISIS large print books.

Details of ISIS complete and unabridged audio books are also available.

Any suggestions for books you would like to see in large print or audio are always welcome.

7 Centremead
Osney Mead
Oxford OX2 0ES
(01865) 250333